Fraud at the Hague-Bakassi

Why Nigeria's Bakassi Territory Was Ceded to Cameroon

Adebayo Adeolu

iUniverse, Inc.
Bloomington

Fraud at the Hague-Bakassi
Why Nigeria's Bakassi Territory Was Ceded to Cameroon

iUniverse books may be ordered through booksellers or by contacting:

iUniverse
1663 Liberty Drive
Bloomington, IN 47403
www.iuniverse.com
1-800-Authors (1-800-288-4677)

ISBN: 978-1-4620-2271-7 (sc)
ISBN: 978-1-4620-2270-0 (hc)
ISBN: 978-1-4620-2266-3 (ebk)

Library of Congress Control Number: 2011907861

Printed in the United States of America

iUniverse rev. date: 09/14/2011

To all of you who chose to be my enemies, with loving affection; to my friends—you know who you are.

Contents

Chapter One

America Is Attacked

As the sky broke into a beautiful sunrise on September 11, 2001, Americans woke up thinking it was another ordinary day. They were unaware of the horror carefully plotted by Islamic fundamentalists in the name of terrorism. The world was about to witness the unimaginable; not even the great scriptwriters in Hollywood ever envisaged such a horrific science fiction movie.

The different cities and nations around the world had almost passed it as a normal day, as the various time zones had put some countries in the afternoon period.

However, America was just rising from slumber, and at 8:46 a.m. disaster struck when hijackers turned passenger planes filled with innocent travelers into missiles[1] by crashing them into the tallest buildings in New York: the famous World Trade Center with its two twin towers. The event led to the deaths of about 3,000 people, with many jumping to their deaths while escaping the buildings that had burst into flames. Still, about 87 percent managed to escape. This was the most horrifying experience on American soil since the attack on Pearl Harbor in 1941. It brought the magnificent World Trade Center into rubbles. The Pentagon was also attacked, and another plane crashed into a field in Pennsylvania. America was on fire in three different areas simultaneously, leaving confusion and panic in the wake.

---

1 Newsweek 31st January, 2005, p.7

The air was filled with smoke, dust, and the smell of death from burnt bodies. People were shocked to their marrow.

The whole world watched in horror as the news broke on CNN, which was seen around the world. The aftermath of the attack left great damage in the Manhattan district with twenty-three buildings damaged and a quarter of the office spaces destroyed.[2] The terrorist attacks changed America overnight, and brought about a new dramatic dimension to security around all public facilities, the aviation industry, the seaports, train stations, and other strategic sectors in the society.

The world learned about the men behind this wicked crime—Osama bin Laden, his agent Mohammed Atta, and other members of the al-Qaeda network. America's security had been breached, and it was only reasonable that whoever was behind the insane attack had to be caught and punished. Islamic radicals practicing as fundamentalists and fanatics became the face of the new enemy.

Americans had responded and united as one big family with a surge in national unity. The country was draped in flags as the shopping outlet Wal-Mart sold 366,000 flags under a forty-eight-hour period.[3] The nation united as one, killing the mood of partisan politics. The attack had brought to focus the vulnerability of America often seen as a superpower, with the greatest military might and oceanic moats.[3]

Who was going to defend and save America from fanatics from the Middle East and those living in caves in Afghanistan? The mantle of leadership was placed on the son of a former president of the United States of America, George H.W. Bush. It was now time to test the competence of the easygoing gentleman who had virtually no experience at the international level.

On September 11, 2001, President George W. Bush concluded that America was at war. It was a day he showed unusual courage, which brought him a lot of respect from people around the world.

He declared he would defend America and stated that he would make no distinction between terrorists and those who harbored them. He promised to tackle Islamic terrorism, take the war to the enemy, and any state sponsoring terrorists or supplying them with weapons of mass destruction (WMD) would also be tackled *before* they became

---

2 The Economist 19th-25th February, 2005 Survey of New York "After The Fall", p.6

3 The Economist 2nd September, 2006 p.20

a threat. America, he declared, would not wait for the next attack but would swing into action to defend its territorial integrity. This became the "Bush Doctrine." It brought some kind of relief and succor to the American people, giving them a renewed confidence that everything was going to be all right again in the United States of America. In the aftermath of the attack, President Bush got a boost with his approval rating hitting the 90 percent mark, the highest rating ever recorded for a president.

However, as the day progressed, condolence messages started to pour in from all over the world. The Russian president, Vladimir Putin, was the first international leader to speak with Bush after the attacks. Putin declared, "In the name of Russia, I want to say to the American people we are with you."[4]

The American people had turned the worst attack on American soil into the most successful rescue operation in the history of the nation. After the president had visited the scene and made his speech, the mayor of New York City took over. Rudolph Giuliani became the voice of America.

He did the job so well that, every time he spoke, people felt relieved. He comforted Americans even though his words were full of grief. He inspired the whole nation and declared, "Tomorrow New York is going to be here. And we're going to rebuild and we're going to be stronger than we were before … I want the people of New York to be an example to the rest of the world, that terrorism can't stop us."[5]

The following week in America was full of grief as the funerals took place. On the twenty-third of September, Yankee Stadium was host to over 20,000 people for a prayer service, making it the first major public event after the attack. It was a challenge to the government and police force to assure and secure the people at the venue, as people did not yet feel completely safe.[6]

The World Trade Center had been attacked by Muslim terrorists in 1993, but nobody ever dreamt terrorists would hijack passenger planes and crash them into its office towers. It is only insane people who do

---

4 Newsweek, December 2008–February 2009, "Special Issue: How to Fix the World," "Forging a New Partnership." Sergey Lavrov. p.34

5 Time "Mayor of the world". Eric Pooley December 31st, 2001 January 7th, 2002, p. 42.

6 Ibid

such a thing because they lose their lives also. The question that arises on the lips of everyone is this: What are they gaining from such a crime since they also lose their lives?

It is the motive and act that have bothered America and Europe, and many other progressive places.

Psychologists have researched how to unravel the mystery behind the hypnotic brainwashing of men or women into taking their own lives and those of other people for no just cause.

The phenomenon of suicide bombers still remains unexplainable; nobody is able to unravel what exactly they do to the victims who agree to these acts of terrorism.

What is it that makes an individual who never showed traits of radicalism or fundamentalism suddenly change in a few months to become a participant? This mystery has to be unraveled.

President George Bush is on record as being one of the least experienced to occupy the Oval Office of the American president.

During the campaign and through his first few months in office, before the attack on the World Trade Center, skeptics had mocked him for his easygoing ways. They imagined this showed shallowness in his working style and views of the world beyond America. Simply put, George W. Bush is the old-fashioned conservative American man from a good family, thoroughbred and refined with a cocky, innocent self-assurance that radiates confidence.[7]

He is a man secretly admired by his treacherous detractors.

A good leader does not need a Harvard vocabulary, and what any nation around the world needs is a commander-in-chief that is clear in his mission and simple enough in his speech for little kids to understand what he is talking about.

The attack of September 11, 2001, on the American nation and its people brought out another side of the president that was not known to the American people before.

It might take a decade or two before they fully understand what President George W. Bush did for the American nation.

President Bush had, however, swung into action. On the way forward to restoring American pride, he used his instincts. Trusting his team, he unleashed a new kind of war against a new kind of enemy.

---

7 Time, "Inside the War Room". James Carney and John F. Dickerson, December 31st 2001/ January 7th 2002 p.70

On September 12, 2001, he summoned the best foreign policy experts ever assembled, including George Tenet, the director of the Central Intelligence Agency (CIA). As the president planned a second visit to New York, on the fourth of October, 2001, after the attack, he had just gone through the *Washington Times* newspaper, where he was taken aback by a story that described all his strategic plans on how the CIA and Pentagon planned to move against the terrorist camps in Afghanistan, including detailed maps. This came as a rude shock to him. Who was leaking confidential and sensitive defense information to the press? Who in turn published it in the daily newspaper as if it was a social event?

President Bush was so disappointed. When Karl Rove and Karen Hughes, the two top advisers, came to his office, he angrily declared "that an act of treason was committed in the newspaper this morning." He made this remark because the White House under his administration had closely monitored and controlled delicate information, which had not been very restricted in previous years.[8]

He thereby called four top congressional leaders to inform them on how he had ordered the FBI, CIA, and Pentagon to reduce the number of lawmakers eligible for classified information concerning the war.

President Bush, without consulting Congress, increased the powers of federal law-enforcement agencies. He reduced the attorney-client privilege for suspected terrorists and introduced martial law to try suspected terrorist in military tribunals. The Arabs were feeling the heat because the problem came from the Middle East countries. He restricted historians from getting classified and sensitive information from the presidential papers.

The United States' president had a leadership role to play in trying times, ranging from economic to that of a war period, and the basic instinct of a good leader is to bring all onboard.

The Republicans and Democrats had to work together for the greater interest of America.

As the speaker of the House, Dennis Hastert invited the president to Congress, saying they were going to give him the resources he would need to wage a war once he could lay down his plans and vision.

President Bush had realized that in government, politicians were

---

8 Ibid

mainly of two groups: those who support you and allow things to work your way and the other group, which he described as obstructionist.

President George Bush had been open and transparent on the cost on the American nation and people in fighting the terrorists. He had told the people of America it could take years, that people would become impatient, that there would be possible setbacks, and that it was not going to be easy because it would cost a lot of blood and treasure.

The president had used his instincts, judgment, principles, and values and was able to create a surge of American patriotism. Any president who expressed the determination to punish enemies of America and proclaimed American values often got the support of the American people.[9] President Bush had gotten all these qualities. However, where these leadership qualities came from still amazes many to date. But not everybody eventually agreed with the measures he took, which seemed to isolate America, creating suspicion and bad blood. But again, time will tell whether his strategy was the right thing or not.

Great leaders who have made notable imprints on the sands of time never folded their arms when faced with difficult challenges or threats. After the September 11, 2001, attack on the World Trade Center, Osama bin Laden, head of the al-Qaeda terrorist organization, announced himself, claiming responsibility for the attacks on the American nation.

He made televised broadcasts and had earlier issued *fatwas* claiming that Islam was under attack by the infidel. He urged Muslims to wage holy war, *jihad,* in its defense. America was deemed the special target for having invaded Arab heartland.[10]

Bin Laden further declared that he was inspired to attack the World Trade Center because of the Israeli bombardment of Beirut in 1982. He said, "As I looked at those destroyed towers in Lebanon, it occurred to me to punish the oppressors in kind by destroying towers in America, so that America would have a taste of its own medicine."[11]

This had led the American president, George W. Bush, to take immediate action by locating the terrorist leader. It was discovered that Osama bin Laden was operating in Afghanistan and had the full support of the Taliban regime. The American government had politely

---

9 Ibid

10 The Economist, September 2nd, 2006, p. 9.

11 Ibid

asked for the Taliban regime to hand him over, but they refused. The Taliban government probably felt intoxicated with power by the fact that the Soviet Union was forced to withdraw from Afghanistan in the 1980s; they felt no superpower could defeat them because of the desert-like and difficult terrain. It was a nation filled with caves and rocks coupled with nasty weather, which exhausted people very easily, especially those who were not from the area.

This gave the Taliban the courage to defy the only superpower left on the world stage. Terrorists had been battering America for a while, but America had not responded or retaliated under previous governments that used diplomacy and counted their losses.

The World Trade Center had once been bombed in 1993, a terrorist attack on American soil, but with less magnitude.

The American embassies in Tanzania and Kenya were attacked and bombed on August 7, 1998. More than 220 innocent people were killed, their lives cut short for no valid reason.

On the twenty-fifth of August, again in 1998, an American franchise restaurant, Planet Hollywood, was bombed in Cape Town, South Africa. The American people had kept their cool.

The attack on America on September 11, 2001, however, was the beginning of a no-nonsense government ready to restore the pride of America and make its people safe.[12]

The failure of the Taliban regime to hand over Osama bin Laden led to the invasion of Afghanistan by the United States of America. The United States got the approval of the international community.

The fighting ended swiftly in favor of the United States' government, and by 2004 a free and fair election had taken place in Afghanistan for the first time ever. It installed and legitimized the presidency of Hamid Karzai. The government, however, continues to be threatened by the Taliban fighters who are mounting pressure in the far south of the state. Afghanistan is known for its opium trade and "warlordism," making it a very unstable country. President Bush had succeeded in installing a more conservative government that would put a stop to terrorist activities in Afghanistan, which had been a former base to plan and launch attacks on the United States.[13]

---

12 BBC Focus on Africa, July–September 2006, The Long War, Nick Ericsson, p. 25

13 Ibid

The success of the United States in Afghanistan only angered the terrorist leader of al–Qaeda, and he kept moving into different countries within the Middle East, making regular television broadcasts to the annoyance of the American government. It was obvious many Middle East countries gave him backing and funding, and many aided him by allowing him free access within their borders and cities.

The Saudis had used their big cash from fabulous oil wealth to fund and advance the cause of Islam. Arab money was given to al–Qaeda, which had spread their network into every nook and cranny of the world. Anywhere there were Muslims, al-Qaeda penetrated while preaching Wahabism, a new kind of message that was at odds with traditional Islamic values and ethics. They preached violence as the solution to societal problems that could have been solved by diplomacy and negotiations.

Islam is the dominant religion of the Arab world. It had started out as Muhamedan, and the people in this new religion called themselves Muhamedan; the practice of worship was called Muhamedanism. It came from the Arab world where the prophet Mohammed taught a new religion and practice of worshipping God, who was known as Allah the supreme God. The people are called Moslems or Muslims. The religion is more popularly called Islam today.[14]

The al-Qaeda network had spread all over Africa, including the northern parts with Algeria, Morocco, Tunisia and other Arab territories, and it was getting a foothold on the west African region.

Peter Chalk of the Jamestown foundation noted that the Armed Islamic group (AIG) in Algeria, the Tuareg insurgency in Mali, the Casa Mance struggle in Senegal, and the religious clashes between Muslims and Christians in Nigeria were aiding the foothold of al-Qaeda on the African continent, which could become a terrorist breeding ground and pose a threat to Western countries.

It was the continued broadcast of Osama bin Laden that led to the invasion of Iraq. It was discovered also that fifteen of the nineteen hijackers on September 11 were born in Saudi Arabia. Iraq as a nation had a radical disposition to the United States and had blown hot air, oftentimes challenging the American government. This had marked the state as one member of the "axis of evil," as defined by President

---

14 Gunther John, Inside Africa, Hamish Hamilton Ltd. London. Published Great Britain, 1955. p.60

George W. Bush. He believed that Iraq possessed weapons of mass destruction (WMD), which were never found after the invasion. But what was gained was freedom for the Iraqi people who had been ruled by Saddam Hussein's tyrannical dictatorship from July 16, 1979, to April 9, 2003, a period of twenty-four years.

Saddam Hussein had run a secular kind of dictatorship, in which Islamists of all stripes and shades kept a low profile.

The American and British governments helped to topple Hussein and organized free elections. The invasion of Iraq had brought back memories of colonialism, and the Iraqis did not want that anymore. Many Muslims and non-Muslims saw the invasion as a way for America to grab the Iraqi people's oil deposits. But the fundamental question is this: Are they taking it for free? The answer is *No*. The oil would be paid for and the funds would be used to develop Iraq and better the lot of the people. Any nation that had a commodity and was cut off from international trade would be on the footnote of decline.

Iraq, as one of the emerging economies in the world and the Middle East, needed the patronage of America and the world. All nations have to engage in favorable international trade to survive. Trade is necessary because no nation is self-sufficient. This creates wealth, which, in turn, is used to develop the state's infrastructures, including roads, houses, water projects, hospitals, schools, and industries, which creates employment. International trade also brings in new innovations like communications systems from around the world, and this advances the status of the people in the society. It raises the literacy levels. Taking the cable television industry that CNN, BBC, Al Jazeera, and others created, this has brought enlightenment to people around the world, including the West: America and Europe. It brings about knowledge, allowing people to see what happens around the world through the news networks.

The citizens of emerging economies in Africa, Asia, and the Middle East, which have been controlled by autocratic regimes, need to increase their literacy levels so they can become more enlightened. Keeping and subduing a people from Western education brings backwardness to them as they are controlled by religious beliefs.

Getting parents and guardians to allow their girls and women to have an education is still an ongoing exercise in many developing countries, including my home country of Nigeria.

Many Muslim-dominated areas have in the past, and some still restrict, women from Western education. These structured restrictions have to be gradually dismantled.

America and European nations have never been the enemy. People all over the world should be grateful for the development and creativity the Western nations have brought to the different parts of the world. The area of medicine cannot be overemphasized as researchers continue to fight disease all over the world by developing and improving the medicines that keep the human race running. The belief that America only came for the oil in Iraq is false and could be regarded as shallow thinking.

If a nation has a mineral or is blessed with oil that has no purchaser, then it becomes untapped and redundant, and that brings no benefit to the nation. The oil or minerals found in any nation becomes a curse or blessing if not properly utilized for the benefit of the people and state where it is found.

President George W. Bush invaded Iraq in March 2003 as the threat by terrorists increased. Iraq was seen as an unfriendly nation toward America, and possibly harboring and funding members of the al-Qaeda network.

President Bush had felt there were weapons of mass destruction in Iraq, but, after the invasion and overthrow of Saddam Hussein, it was discovered that there was no link to al-Qaeda or biological or chemical WMDs. It was an unfortunate action, which only shows clearly that propaganda and aggressive behaviors toward other nations can actually convince the world that a nation might be capable of having what it does not even have the knowledge to build. Most nations had honestly felt Iraq had acquired superpower weapons; even Africans had the belief and fear that Iraq had become one of the countries with the nuclear capability.

America went in easily and captured Saddam Hussein to the horror and fear of other nations. Nations around the world started feeling uncomfortable at seeing America as an imperialist nation bullying weaker nations and forcing them into submission.

The United Nations had not approved and given the United States of America the mandate for war. The invasion breached the United Nations mandate for the approval to invade Iraq and led to a division in the Security Council. America and Britain stood on one side while France, Germany, Russia, and China were not in agreement.

As the claims that weapons of mass destruction had existed in Iraq finally became false, Muslims around the world and Christians began to assume that this had been just a pretext to get Iraq's oil. The British prime minister had defended the action, saying the invasion was to support Islamic moderates against reactionaries and to support democracy against the draconian dictatorship rule.

However, once Saddam Hussein was toppled, the American and British governments helped to organize free and fair elections, promoting a free society tailored to democratic values and principles. This was good, but many people in countries around the world still kept asking: What right did America and Britain have to invade someone else's country in order to impose a pattern of government there?

Critics of America's role in promoting democracy and free societies around the world don't have the knowledge of what it is to be a refugee, talk less of experiencing it. The problems that come with bad leadership arise oftentimes from autocratic rule, which often leads to civil unrest that escalates into civil wars. This wakes up the tribal sentiments within the society, which often leads to ethnic cleansing where the tribal leader targets other ethnic groups within his society.

The next phase becomes genocide within the nation, which often leads to the mass exodus of people who become displaced overnight and assume refugee status. People flee from political persecution and harm around the world, including Somalia, Congo, Kenya, Rwanda, Zimbabwe, Liberia, Uganda, and Kosovo. Many of these countries have become failed states and need the intervention of Western nations.

The September 11, 2001, attacks shocked the Arab psyche, and initially the Muslims were in denial and angered by the unfolding events. Many initially authored the belief that it could have been a Mossad plot by the Israelis. They eventually realized the dysfunction in the world of Islam, where the woes within the Arab and Middle East countries were blamed on others.[15]

In 2001, some Muslims shared bin Laden's feeling as they cheered on the attacks that took place in America. CNN even featured uninformed youths cheering in Kano state, Nigeria. These are the results of the low level of literacy found around the world.

---

15 Newsweek, July 18th, 2005, p. 25.

Muhammad Hussein Fadlallah, the most popular Shiite cleric in Lebanon, however, disagreed with the terrorist approach of solving issues. He declared that whatever differences they had with America and its democratic drive in the Middle East, the situation did not warrant criminal and barbaric behavior. He said the September 11, 2001, attacks on the United States were a stain on Islam.

Another conference took place in Jordan where 180 top Muslim clerics and imams, brought together under the auspices of Jordan's King Abdulla, declared that no Muslim be declared an *apostate-takfir*. This was the al-Qaeda method preferred by bin Laden and his ally in Iraq, Abu Mussab al Zarqawi. Ten fatwas were issued by conservative scholars, including, Iraq's grand ayatollah Ali Sistani, Egypt's mufti Ali Juma, and the popular and influential Yusuf al-Qaradawi of Al Jazeera's popular program *TV Sheik,* and were signed by adherents of all schools of *fiqh* (Islamic jurisprudence).

The Islamic conference had stated that only qualified Muslim scholars could issue edicts. This was unity among scholars to denounce the terrorists.

That very day al-Qaeda in Iraq declared that the Egyptian ambassador to Iraq, Ihab al-Sherif, would be killed as an apostate. That only confirmed the struggle going on within Islam as a religion: the radical fundamentalist group against the conservative Muslims who abide by the Muslim law and the Koran.

The next day, July 7, 2005, was the day the London bombing took place, and simultaneously a message from Zarqawi's group was placed on the Internet. It said they had killed the "ambassador of the infidels."[16]

The July 7 bombing was the bloodiest day in Britain since the Second World War ended. Britain was, however, not at war with anybody. They only supported America to condemn terrorism. Prime Minister Tony Blair had done the right thing by giving support to America. The early 1970s and middle 1990s had witnessed terrorist attacks in Britain from the Irish Republic Army (IRA), but they were more humane to warn the public before setting of any bomb.

There had been a bombing by terrorists in Madrid Spain sixteen months earlier where ten trains were attacked. This took place on the eleventh of March, 2004. Al-Qaeda posted explicit notices on extremist

16 Ibid

websites, saying they would "create waterfalls of blood."[17] These acts further triggered a determination to tackle the war on terror.

The al-Qaeda network began recruiting European passport holders who could enter the United States without a visa, and they recruited Muslims within the European Union and Britain. These are second and third generation Muslims who were born in Europe and whose parents were immigrants after the Second World War. After 1945, Germany and many other European countries opened their borders to an influx of foreigners who wanted to have a better life in Europe, which offered better opportunities as more developed societies. The immigrants had come from Morocco, Algeria, Tunisia, Egypt, Libya, and other North Africa states. That was how the Muslim religion penetrated into Europe.

The London bombing targeted the mass transit system. Two tube trains were hit at Edgware Road, leading to seven deaths at 8:50 a.m. The second bomb went off at Tavistock Square 9:47 a.m. A popular London double-decker, bus 30, was the target, ripping the roof open in mangled iron shreds. This caused the deaths of thirteen people. Another bomb hit the deep tube at Russell Square; over twenty-one people died. Then the last attack took place at Aldgate, about a hundred yards from Liverpool Street. Seven people died. The bombings were targeted to also undermine the G8 conference of the leaders of the industrialized nations, which was taking place in Scotland.

Despite the horror, carnage, and deaths resulting from the terror attacks, al-Qaeda got emboldened, and, not yet satisfied, they continued with threats. This led to the straw that broke the camel's back when bin Laden started targeting Muslim countries from Indonesia to Morocco, Kenya, Turkey, etc. This was an eye opener for Muslims who realized they were being targeted, and this took the shine from the star of Osama bin Laden.

The bombing of Muslim nations now convinced other world powers they all had a problem. India, Pakistan, Europe, Asia, Russia, China, and Japan now became united and in agreement with the United States to defeat the Taliban and put in place a government that would not support al-Qaeda and its terrorist acts.

The world powers still felt some unease with the way America had singlehandedly gone into two independent countries within the Middle

17 Newsweek, August 9th, 2004, p. 17

East, defying the United Nations, which had not given them the go-ahead or approval, especially with the case of Iraq.

It was an eye opener for many people as they felt threatened by the way President Bush barked out orders, saying people were either with him or on the other side. President Bush had said, "The best hope for peace in our world is expansion of freedom in all the world." He further declared that promoting freedom was now American policy. This statement sent shivers down the spines of dictators around the world who became cautious with the way they governed their independent states. Washington seemed to be spreading its ideals with the barrel of a gun.

A former French minister exclaimed that the United States was the last "Bismarckian power" that believed military power was the best instrument of foreign policy.[18]

The United States of America is a big country packaged with military, economic, and political dominance. It remains the only superpower of the world. America, despite all its military might, is still threatened by faceless Islamic terrorist organizations who are small and minorities, but small groups can cause big damage if unchecked.

The United Nations and World Bank were created after the Second World War ended in 1945 to create and enforce world peace and later to deal with poverty in poor countries and to fight inequality. However, when America defied the United Nations Security Council and acted unilaterally, there was an outcry among world leaders—not for the fact that Iraq was invaded, but because they were afraid America was behaving like a hegemonic imperialist power, which they last saw in the days of Nazi Germany.

America's new foreign policy approach had affected some countries positively because, while America concentrated on fighting the war on terror, it had given Asian countries an edge by giving them strategic space. The Chinese economy doubled and Beijing's global influence took world stage.

America today controls space and information technology and grabs critical geographic points around the world. The United States provides public goods like free trade, technological innovation, and safe sea lanes, and it creates regional stability around the world.

---

18 Dream on, America, Andrew Moravcsik, Newsweek January 31st, 2005, p.31

The other G8 members would have preferred the multilateral approach where common rules agreed by all are the most effective means to secure respect from other members. Meaning, when common rules are broken or ignored, the violator must pay a price or be sanctioned. This integrates tomorrow's new powers into reviewed international order, promotes economic growth, fights global poverty, and preserves the environment. The same goes for the threats faced by all from radical Islamists. The United States must, however, trust Europe by working together using multilateralism.

However, despite the unilateral decision America made when it invaded Iraq without the United Nations Security Council's approval, many world leaders would not want America to withdraw from playing its role as a global leader that brings stability around the world. America has acted for decades as big brother to many nations who are threatened by political or economic factors.[19]

America played this role when Saddam Hussein invaded Kuwait (1990–1991), a stronger nation annexing a weaker one without a just cause. President George H.W. Bush pushed Iraq out of Kuwait and the United States played its special role as a force for global order. The American Congress had been reluctant at the time, but Bush had countered the aggressive power grab from Iraq, restoring Kuwait's sovereignty.

Osama bin Laden continued to threaten all the countries that were supporting America on the war on terror, especially all who contributed by sending troops to Afghanistan and Iraq, even where they were peace-keeping forces. The Italians sent about 3,000 troops and Denmark sent 530, but all felt the threat.

Most refugee migrants landed in Italy illegally from the Middle East via Libya. There was the need to block the movement of extremists because they could take advantage of the route to get into Europe. Terrorists were going to be governed by new laws different from law-abiding citizens.

The Italian prime minister had triggered Muslim resentment when he made certain statements after the September 11, 2001, attacks popularly referred to as "the 9/11 attack on America." He lauded the "superiority" of Western civilization. A statement issued after the London bombs declared Rome a target, calling it a "collaborating

19 Newsweek, "Special Edition/Issue 2008."

government" and "capital of infidels." The Muslims identified the Italian prime minister, Silvio Berlusconi, as the third B. The policy of the "three B's Bush, Blair and Berlusconi."[20]

Following the al-Qaeda threats, France suspended the free movement accord from the Schengen Visa. Nations across the world tightened the security at the airports, seaports, etc. The assault from the terrorists spurred vigilance; passengers wishing to board an aircraft must now queue to remove their shoes, belts, and all metal objects for proper screening. Tougher cockpit doors have been built on planes, and stricter immigration rules, such as disclosure of every country a traveler has visited in the last ten years, help screen out potential terrorists before they reach the American soil.[21]

On the morning of September 11, 2001, President Bush was reading *My Pet Goat* to a class of second graders, which demonstrated his good, simple nature.

President Bush soon invaded Afghanistan and Iraq, thereby making America safer so that the terrorists are kept outside the United States. Whether we agree or not, President George W. Bush made America safer. I think Americans should have realized this fact by now.

---

20 The Economist, July 16th, 2005. Special Report Muslim Extremism in Europe

21 Ibid

Chapter Two

The Islamic Revolution

President Franklin D. Roosevelt of the United States of America hastily declared to Winston Churchill of Britain that the Atlantic Charter of 1941, which they had drawn up together, should not only apply to the conquered nations of Europe, but it should be extended to the British territories and colonies in Africa.

He said it was the right of all peoples to choose their governments. He wanted post-war objectives to include self-determination for all colonial peoples.

In 1943, Roosevelt had a brief stopover in Gambia on his way to the Casablanca conference. Shocked by the backwardness and poverty, he described the place as a "hell hole" and told Sultan Mohammed V that the Atlantic Charter applied to Morocco as well as all other colonies, bringing about nationalism in Morocco and elsewhere. This annoyed both the British and French who saw it as the interference of America trying to meddle with their territories and internal domestic policies.[22]

Roosevelt had not known these regions of Africa and peoples and had probably likened their ways and lifestyles to the developed world of America and Europe.

He had not gone inside Africa, to the interior areas, to understand

---

22 Martin Meredith The State of Africa, A History of Fifty Years of Independence, Great Britain, Free Press, 2005. p. 9

the complexity and intricacies woven around the different colonial states that were still bedeviled by superstition, ethnicity, cannibalism, slavery, and many barbaric and backward cultures and customs.

They still needed the reformation and modernization that the Western cultures had overcome centuries ago. Many of the African states were not ready for self-government and independence. The structures were just not there.

This hasty decision brought about instability and the collapse of Africa that continues today, which is plagued by internal wars, famine, poverty, refugee problems, and genocide, just to mention a few.

Liberia was founded as a result of freed slaves from the United States of America in 1847.[23] Ethiopia was never colonized. It had always been Christian indigenously. It was annexed by Italy between 1936–41 and was restored to Haile Selassie who returned from exile.

The Union of South Africa was the richest state in Africa at the time, due to mineral deposits such as gold. It was given independence in 1910 under white minority rule. And Egypt was ruled by King Farouk who emerged from a Turkish dynasty of 140 years. But the events of July 23, 1952, changed all that, forcing him to abdicate his throne and go on exile.

The army officers who executed the coup called themselves the Revolutionary Command Council (RCC). They purged the state of all former loyalists to the Farouk dynasty. The monarchy was abolished and, in the attempt for popular support, formed the political movement called the Liberation Rally. Colonel Nasser was nominated as the secretary-general, and through the position he emerged from the shadows as Egypt's new leader.

Nasser then began negotiations with Britain to pull their military base out of Egypt and the Canal Zone, which was an indispensable part of Britain's global interest. This was the largest overseas armed forces base in the world that monitored the sea routes of Europe, Asia, and Africa. The Egyptian government had finally convinced Britain to pull out by October 1954. Britain effected the agreement on the eighteenth of June, 1956.

Nasser consolidated his position as leader in Egypt by using repressive force to silence the opposition. He gradually became a

23 Gunther John, Inside Africa, London, Hamish Hamilton Ltd. 1954, p. 30,31.

dictator. In 1955, Israel struck the Egyptian military garrison in the Gaza Strip, which led to a war. Nasser attempted to buy arms and weapons from the Western governments, but they turned him down so he reached out to the Russians who obliged him. Tankers and fighter jets were purchased in exchange for cotton.

This threatened Britain and America, especially because Nasser was opening the British sphere of political interest, influence, and power to the opposition. Russia had little influence in the Middle East and Africa politically, which was the domain of Western influence.

The next step Nasser took was to nationalize the Suez Company, which was owned by the British and French. The Suez Canal, constructed in 1866, was commercially the world's most important seaway. It hosted about 12,000 ships yearly from about forty-seven countries; all important commercial cargo passed through the canal, carrying everything from raw materials to finished products and oil.

The Suez Canal put Nasser and Britain in conflict, which resulted in Her Majesty's government striking Egypt. Nasser retaliated by sinking forty-seven ships, which blocked the Suez Canal and disrupted commercial trade, leading to petroleum shortages. Britain had to withdraw further hostilities.

This event brought Nasser to fame in the Arab world, marking the beginning of the Arab revolution.

Nasser practiced Arab socialism as against Western-style capitalism.

The next country and state to defy the West was Libya. Colonel Muammar Gaddafi had emerged as president of Libya in a military coup in 1969. He was just a twenty-seven-year-old signal officer driven by the cult of Nasser. He had the grand ambition and ultimate desire of ruling all Africa in his made-up world where the United States of Africa would emerge under his leadership. It was the reason he meddled in the affairs of other countries, ever hoping to bring them under his control. He used the huge revenues from oil reserves to acquire arms and weapons of mass destruction: fighter jets, submarines, tanks, helicopters, etc. He often intimidated other leaders by bringing a huge armory from Libya to accompany him on state visits to other countries in Africa.

He also did the same as Nasser in Egypt. He got rid of British and American military bases in Libya and nationalized foreign-owned property and business interests. He reviewed the legal code to include *Sharia* law and formed the Arab socialism, all offshoots of the Nasser governing style. Anything Western was rejected; churches were closed down; nightclubs and alcohol became illegal. He published *The Green Book,* which has three parts and is used as recommended text for all students.

Colonel Gaddafi, on assuming the leadership position in Libya, introduced the Tripoli Charter in 1970, which intended to merge Egypt, Libya, and Sudan together.

In 1971 came another treaty, forging Libya, Egypt, and Syria together, called the Benghazi Treaty. In 1973 another accord was formed with Algeria, and this one became known as the Messaoud Accords. In 1974 Libya struck still another accord with Tunisia: the Djerba Treaty.

All the accords for greater Arab unity fell through; nobody wanted Gaddafi because he was just too overbearing and radical. Successive governments in Egypt disdained the alliances, especially Anwar al Sadat.

By 1976, Gaddafi fell out of favor with President Numeiri of Sudan who had accused Libya of funding the coup plot to overthrow him in Khartoum. Similar situations followed in Tunisia and Algeria.

Gaddafi got blacklisted by Arab neighbors in a diplomatic way, and this made him more determined and ruthless, which led to his subversive methods of using oil funds to support dissidents, militants, and insurgent groups. He wanted to deal with those who opposed him or did not share his views, including opposition leaders who had gone into exile. He was feared by opponents for his treacherous and ruthless style.

He influenced thirty African governments to break ties with Israel, including Nigeria at the time. He also sponsored the Palestinian course against Israel, the IRA, Basque separatist movement, and other militant groups, etc. Gaddafi had been involved over the years in international terrorism and had built a massive military force, which he used to intimidate weaker African leaders.

Gaddafi spent billions of dollars on arms bought from France, the Soviet Union, and others on the black market, spending a whopping $29 billion between 1970 and 1985. He expanded his territory, taking advantage of the civil war in Chad. This was the period when he occupied the Aozou Strip, which was the border area about 450 miles inside Chad, bringing Libya, directly next door to Chad. This caused disaffection up north in Chad. One faction that obviously got patronage from Libya did not mind the occupation. It was led by Goukouni Queddi. The other faction involved in the conflict within the border of Chad that struggled for control was opposed to Libya. It was led by Hissein Habre. He was forced out of northern Chad and moved south.

Gaddafi then sponsored another dissident group called the Volcan Army, all three forces combined together. The Volcan Army and Goukouni Queddi, who wanted to overthrow General Malloum, had combined with Habre. France was invited in at the peak of the hostilities, and they destroyed Gaddafi's men: the Volcan Army along with Goukouni. The rift brought instability to Chad. It was Nigeria, Sudan, Niger, and France that tried to mediate. Even Libya was in the mediation team, pretending to have clean hands.

Goukouni was chosen as president and Habre became the minister of defense. Kamougue, a colonel, became vice president. Clashes, however, continued between northerners and southerners. Finally, in 1980, Gaddafi sent Libyan troops backed by tanks and heavy artillery with Islamic warriors who joined Goukouni's forces to drive Habre's fighters out of the capital, forcing Habre to seek refuge in Sudan.

By 1981, Gaddafi announced a merger with Chad; automatically he craftily annexed Chad. This led to an uproar around the other African states and the world.

The country continued to have problems. There was a country and population but no government authority. The whole country was destabilized and in ruins; schools and hospitals were converted to houses by miscreants.

For two decades, Libya sponsored insurrectionist groups inside Chad. That was until the Americans stepped in by helping Habre on the sixteenth of December, 1986. The Libyans were defeated. Many were slaughtered, and the remaining fled, abandoning their equipment worth over a billion dollars. Gaddafi's dream came tumbling down like a pack of cards. He also lost the Aozou Strip, which he fraudulently claimed belonged to Libya. He had used an unratified treaty between Italy and France in 1935 to make the false claim.

Gaddafi got so disgruntled that he decided to punish France and

America. In 1988, just two years after Libya shot down Pan Am flight 103 over Lockerbie, Scotland, with 270 people, mostly Americans, being killed. The government denied involvement but accepted the involvement of two Libyan citizens.

And the French government too was punished when a French UTA jetliner was bombed midair over Niger in 1989. Another 170 people perished. Sannusi Abdullah was convicted a decade later *in absentia* in a French court as the mastermind. He was among the intelligence officers and also a brother-in-law to Gaddafi.

However, despite all the odds from the past, it can be seen that the moves by former president George W. Bush of America to deal with terrorists had worked. They reduced the boldness of the Islamist terrorists as he invaded Afghanistan and defeated the Taliban government promptly. He also went into Iraq and got Saddam Hussein out of the place. This sent a clear signal to long-sitting presidents who had sponsored terrorism across the globe. Gaddafi knew and felt the heat that he would be next.

In March 2003, one of Gaddafi's closest associates, Musa Kusa, the much feared head of Libya's foreign intelligence service, the Jamahariya Security Organization (JSO), and Saif Al Islam, Gaddafi's son, went cap in hand to the British government to inform them that Gaddafi was ready to come transparent. He would disclose his weapons of mass destruction programs in exchange for assurances that his regime would be spared from destruction and humiliation.

Gaddafi finally abandoned his nuclear ambitions when the Americans presented him with a compact disc made by the United States' National Security Agency of an intercepted conversation between the head of Libya's nuclear program, Maatouq Mohammed Matouq, and Abdul Qadeer Khan, the now discredited head of Pakistan's nuclear program who ran a clandestine black market in nuclear equipment.

The British government and Americans accepted the offer with Gaddafi promising $10 million to each family member that had lost someone on the Pan Am flight 103 over Lockerbie Scotland. It totaled $2.7 billion.[24]

The West lifted sanctions on Libya when Gaddafi surrendered

24 The Middle East, July 2006 Issue 369 Arabs Wage War on Money Laundering The Libyan Connection, Ed Blanche, p. 20.

two of his intelligence officers for trial for the 1988 for bombing of the American jet.

Sudan

The most notorious of the Arab states of North Africa for harboring and accommodating terrorists is the Sudan. The Sudanese government has been brought to global focus by all the happenings around its genocidal war against the south. Sudan is the largest country in Africa, and at independence in 1956 the north gained control. The north of Sudan, including Khartoum, is more advanced than the southern parts. The north had been in close interaction with the Middle Eastern Arab countries, resulting in their advanced society.

Sudan can be divided into three regions: the north (with Khartoum, the capital), Darfur, and the south.

The north is dominated by the Muslim Arab elite of the Nile who had gained control from the time of independence. It is the seat of government and the most developed region in Sudan. In fact, it has been remodeled in the capital city to a replica of Dubai.

Darfur, on the other hand, is a very poor region and has been neglected by the ruling elite of the north over the years. It is very remote and had almost been forgotten by the British colonial government. It was a difficult region to access at the time of colonial rule and was not included into the colony of Britain until 1916.

Darfur is home to about six million people, but the area has been turned into a mass graveyard: over two million killed and about 1.6 million displaced from their homes and farms, all facing starvation and hunger as the conflicts cause them to miss the planting season. The Sudanese central government has been at war with Darfur rebels who feel they should have more revenue allotted to them in the region.

The ruling elite and Arab Islamic Muslims up north have resisted their demands for decades, and the fighting continues as Arabs kill Arabs. The ruling elite are just as black as the indigenous black Africans in Darfur or their Arab counterparts. The Africans in Darfur are Muslim, but, despite this, they are slaughtered by government-sponsored rebels from the north. These rebels are Janjaweed Arab militiamen who bomb and, riding horses and camels burn down houses, rob, rape, and kill the black civilians who have the audacity to ask for more revenues. The central government says it is fighting rebels in Darfur, but everybody is affected.

The Darfur rebels have only asked for more funds to develop the area and are angry after years of neglect. They decided that if the southerners in Sudan can win a share of power by taking up arms, so can they. The government, on the other hand, feels uneasy that giving concessions to Darfur will tempt other restless regions to rebel.

The south of Sudan got the same treatment as Darfur—evidence of the economic boom outside the capital city of Khartoum is hard to find. The irony of it all is that the oil wealth comes from the south of Sudan. The central government laid oil pipes all the way to the north and controls and manipulates all the revenues from the vast oil reserves. The other regions—Darfur and south Sudan—have electricity problems, and some schools still hold classes under trees.

The south has 80 percent of the oil found in Sudan.[25]

The south is inhabited by Christian and animist black Africans who have been in rebellion against the Arab north, asking for a greater share of the wealth and self-rule. They want to be independent. The region holds the key to development in Sudan. John Garang, now late, had led the rebellion in southern Sudan for twenty-two years. He was killed in a helicopter crash in 2005.[26]

The government in Khartoum created the Arab militia known as Janjaweed, the horse-riding Islamist militants. Musa Hilal, a Janjaweed leader, is believed to have a strong army of about 12,000 fighters loyal to him. It would be difficult to control him as senior military officers treat him with respect. He shuttles between Khartoum and Darfur and always defends his actions by saying he is protecting Arabs. The latest ideology is the supremacy of the Arabs. In Darfur *Arab* has become like a political label.[27]

The Islamic revolution that took place in Iran on January 16, 1979, brought an end to the government of the shah of Iran. Ayatollah Khomeini had returned from exile in France and was received by large crowds of about five million Iranians.

This marked the beginning of Iran's theocracy, an aberration and departure from centuries of Sunni thought. It was the beginning of the

25 The Economist, August 5, 2006, p. 36.

26 The Economist, August 6, 2005, p. 11.

27 The Economist, July 31, 2004, p. 32.

Wahhabi mindset, which brought the rule of the clerics and a new form of extremism opposed to Western governments.

The influence of Iran, which was part of the Middle East, had put Shiite mullahs in charge. The new regime pledged its support for Islamist movements everywhere. Thus began the influence that sneaked into Iraq but was put in check by the late Saddam Hussein. It began to forge its way in the Middle East in places like Afghanistan, Lebanon, and Saudi Arabia, and eventually got hold of North Africa.

The African continent can be divided into two: the north, which has countries like Morocco, Algeria, Tunisia, and Egypt, which are closely related with southern Spain, Greece, and Turkey. They are Mediterranean countries much closer to Europe than to black Africa. It is a belief and trend that above the Sahara Desert, Africa is *Europe,* and below the desert *Africa is Africa.*

The North Africans tend to be lighter skinned, which resulted from the profuse admixture of peoples that still occurs till date· Hamitic Ethiopians have crossed with Semitic Arabs, Berbers have crossed with Negroes from the French Sudan, and Negroes and Bantu are extricably commingled in the Congo, Nigeria, and elsewhere.

The other countries with Arabs and Islamic codes in Africa are Mauritania, Libya, Sudan, Djibouti, and Somalia. They call themselves Arabs even though the black Negroes live among them.

The five European powers t hat ruled and colonized Africa and who created the scramble for African territories are Britain, France, Belgium, Portugal, and Spain. Germany joined later and was excluded from owning territories in Africa after the First World War.

North African states adopted radical Islam in the last two decades, heavily influenced by the Middle East that had support them with surplus funds from oil income.[28]

Osama bin Laden had relocated to Africa sometime in 1991 making Sudan his new home. It was there he established the al-Qaeda network. Bin Laden's long-term aim was to topple all pro-American or pro-Western regimes in the Muslim world so as to establish a new caliphate.

The Saudi government had given the jihadist a free hand to spread their radical views and theories and had financed them in waging their

---

28 BBC Focus on Africa, July-September 2006, "al-Qaeda in Africa," p. 20

war abroad. But not until bin Laden's network started killing people inside Saudi Arabia did the government wake up to tackle terrorism. Many of the jihadists are in different parts of the world, including Iraq. When they return to Saudi Arabia, they may try to overthrow the government and royal family as was done in Iran in 1979.

Radical Islamist groups are merely creating tension by their terrorist acts and activities. What they really want is to hijack the political and economic control of the various states they have come from by using inflammatory religious beliefs, ideals, and sentiments to topple the Westernized system of government that exists already.[29]

Sudan had become very radical in its religious outlook from the time General Omar al Bashir came to power in 1989. It was the beginning of a new dawn. He had declared that anyone who betrayed the nation would be executed. It was the beginning of an Islamist dictatorship.

All moderate Muslim sects were silenced. He then purged all the arms of government: the legislature, judiciary, civil service, trade unions, etc. Christianity was suppressed, and vocal opposition members were detained and tortured.

The introduction of Sharia became prominent with a new penal code introduced in 1991. It brought draconian justice like public hanging for armed robbers, stoning of adulterers, either male or female, and death for apostasy. The government went as far as banning music, which all races and religions partake in. All cultures of the world have their forms of music. The government placed a ban on men and women dancing together. The police were used as a coercive and oppressive force to break up wedding ceremonies.

The Khartoum government introduced new regulations separating men and women in public transportation, meaning a woman could not go on the same bus with a man. They discouraged Muslim men from looking at women. They encouraged men to grow long beards.

Religion was effectively used as methods of repression and enforcing their own new radical brand of Islam that promoted Arabisation while demeaning other cultures. Bashir created the People's Defence Force (PDF), which was similar to Iran's Revolutionary Guards. The PDF, which had a strength of about 150,000 people, was imposed on the population. It was a movement used to quell civilian disturbances in

29 The Economist, September 2, 2006, p 10.

the form of demonstrations, and the organization was coerced when the government declared it sacred for Muslims to join.

By 1991, during the Gulf War crisis, the Sudanese government had invited militant groups into Sudan to resist the American presence in the Middle East. Islamic militants and terror groups were formed. Many came from Tunisia, Algeria, and Egypt, and they were offered diplomatic passports by the Sudanese government. By the beginning of 1992, there were over a thousand terrorists from Egypt and Palestine. Even Carlos the Jackal who could not get a visa for Iraq and Libya, was accommodated. Osama bin Laden also came to stay in Sudan. It was the meeting point for radicals as the government hosted them. Bin Laden used Sudan as his new base for al-Qaeda. Then he later returned to Saudi Arabia.

When Iraq invaded Kuwait and annexed it, Saudi Arabia felt threatened and uneasy. In 1990, Bin Laden offered to mobilize 10,000 *mujahidin* fighters, but the Saudi government and royal family turned the request down, preferring to invite and use American defense. His ploy to gain popularity failed as the royal family recognized him as a rebel who might foment trouble and overthrow the monarchy.

This annoyed Osama bin Laden, and he now resorted to denouncing the throne of Saudi Arabia. The royal family now sent him on exile, restricting him to Jeddah, which led to this relocation to Sudan. There he continued to criticize the royal family, saying they had moved away from the true path of Islam. He was involved in business in Sudan, from construction to other lucrative deals, and lived next door to the radical Islamic cleric Turabi.

Bin Laden continued to invest in terrorist insurgent groups. He brought in Arab mujahidin from Pakistan to Sudan. He set up training camps where over 5,000 terrorist militants were trained. These activities became known around the world, making Sudan a terrorist state.

The final action that brought sanctions on Sudan was the assassination attempt on President Mubarak of Egypt when he visited Ethiopia. He was attacked at Addis Ababa on his way to attend a summit of the Organization of African Unity. The attackers had crossed the border from Sudan. They were of Egyptian origin.

This assassination attempt exposed General Omar al Bashir as a supporter of terrorism. This dented his image so badly that he asked Osama bin Laden to leave Sudan in March 1996. The general had given him sanctuary for five years, which allowed him to build and position al-Qaeda.

The Arabisation of North Africa and the Islamic terrorists led to many of the crises in different parts of Africa, which came toward the West African region of Africa. The Arab and Islamic influence brought crisis of its own kind in Nigeria, Ivory Coast, Somalia, Congo, Uganda, and a host of other countries.

The theocratic government in Iran has the ambition to be a superpower not only in the Middle East, but also in the entire Muslim world. The Iranian government has used the robust financial wealth it has acquired from oil to induce poor nations and people to project its Islamist fundamentalism.

The government had also brainwashed its people that the shah of Iran, who was liberal and more tolerant, was a creature and creation of the American government. They did this by spreading the false insinuation that America was pro-Israel and anti–Palestine, and indeed anti-Islam, but the older generation of Iranians are beginning to see clearly that the assumptions are false.

It was the activist intellectual that brought the idea of *jihad* to the minds of certain Muslims. It was an ideology of Sayyid Qutb, an Egyptian whose writings influenced generations of radical Islamists. Sayyid Qutb had been trained in the Western European culture, which he admired.

The easygoing gentleman suddenly changed direction after a two-year stay in the United States in the late 1940s. The racial discrimination that was practiced in America did not go down well with him; segregation was enforced in certain states at the time. It is a known fact that many Arabs don't really like Negroes and have for centuries not accepted the fact that Arabs are seen as blacks. The light skin color did not help and only brought more trouble. They were neither black nor white.

The racial conflict of race definition brought the once liberal gentleman into a state of confusion. Segregation restricted him. This led to the hate and radical writings against the West: Europe and America. He then began to look inward, falling back on the Egyptian culture and trying to create core values of their customs and heritage as the *real* way of life.

This led to denouncing Western values and systems. He returned to Egypt in 1951, promoting the culture of people of the Nile, and became a leading figure in the Muslim Brotherhood. Nasser, however, did not accept some of the radical views being preached, and Sayyid Qutb came into conflict with his government.

In 1954, he was accused of attempting to assassinate Nasser. He also divided the Muslim society into two diametrically opposed camps: those belonging to Satan and those belonging to the party of God. He noted that repressive regimes like the one Nasser led as leader in Egypt were unIslamic and that change would not be possible within the borders of the Egyptian state. He therefore said the only way there could be change was the use of jihad, which Prophet Mohammed had used centuries ago.

In 1965, the Muslim Brotherhood was accused and blamed for another attempt to assassinate Nasser. This eventually got Sayyid Qutb executed. However, this brought about the emergence of another radical scholar and cleric: Omar Abdel Rahman, who got his education in Cairo's Al-Azhar University. He became a militant activist even though he was blind. He went on to criticize Nasser, calling him an infidel and an apostate. This provoked the government in Egypt, and Nasser imprisoned him in 1970 for eight months.

After serving his jail term, he was appointed professor of theology at the University of Asyut in 1973. He continued his radical Islamic preaching, which brought followers who had not found a place in the existing structures. They became radical followers in their thinking and looked to the cleric as their spiritual mentor. These revolutionary organizations like Gamaa Islamiya and Jamaat al-Jihad had the desire to establish an Islamic republic.

The threat of radical Islam in North Africa became intensified in the 1980s after the Islamic revolution in Iran in 1979. Nasser's successor, Anwar al Sadat, initially tried to get the support of Islamic groups in order to bolster his own position. He called himself "Believer President." He supported Islamic courses at the time, reaching agreements with the Muslim Brotherhood not to engage in violence. This, however, did not satisfy his Islamic critics who wanted nothing to do with Western countries.

His open-door economic policy, which favored Western interests, and his peace accord with Israel in 1979, which earned him a Nobel Peace Prize did not satisfy his critics.

He also used the military to put a check on troublemakers who called him *pharaoh.*

The Muslim Brotherhood, not wanting anything to do with the Western way of life, had gotten President Sadat to look inward at the ancient culture. So he used a throne-like chair from the ancient and true culture of Egypt on the day he inspected a parade on the sixth of October, 1981. On this day, an Islamic terrorist within the army gunned him down while screaming, "I have killed pharaoh!" He got a light sentence of three years imprisonment.

Jamaat al-Jihad members believe that jihad is the sixth pillar of Islam. The belief was for all true Muslims to correct the ills of a decadent and bad society by the extermination of the infidel leaders who practiced Western forms of government as against the complete Islamic order.

Sadat's successor, Hosni Mubarak, a former air force commander, is today well into his eighties who was the maximum ruler in Egypt has recently been overthrown by people through mass protests instigated by what is now known as a Digital Revolution through social media and internet like Facebook and Twitter. He faced a series of violent challenges with terrorist Muslims. He used outright force and emergency laws to keep a tight grip on running of the Egyptian state. He did not hand over the leadership position for the fear that radical Muslim insurgents might take control of Egypt, making it a Muslim nation.

Tunisia, Morocco, and Libya have also succeeded in crushing the radical groups who have the desire to make all Muslim states like Iran: a government managed and run by Islam. Religious bodies should not form theocratic governments. These are aberrations, and nothing good comes from such systems but repression and oppression committed in the name of God. Religion should be removed from politics and government.

Chapter Three

The Crisis in Africa

Five decades after independence, most of the African countries have proved that the Europeans left too early. Many of the states in Africa had not gotten the needed experience to become independent of the colonial masters.

The colonial masters, on handing over the African continent to the African nationalist elites, had used kind words of advice, saying the new leaders should not compromise the future with hasty reforms, and that the structures that were laid down should not be changed until the new leaders were sure they had better alternatives.

Britain had fourteen African territories, with Ghana and Nigeria among the most advanced states. The colonies of Belgium and France were not as advanced, and the French continued to run their colonies indirectly well after independence as they continued to provide manpower and infrastructure for many years. Ivory Coast was the only advanced French colony.

The African nationalist elite group who had gotten the "golden fleece," as foreign education was called in the last century, did not have much experience in running a young, developing country. Many had gone abroad and acquired educational skills by getting degrees in law, engineering, architecture, medicine, pharmacy, etc.[30] This made

30 Martin Meredith, The State of Africa Fifty Years of Independence, Free Press, London, 2005. p.11

them *feel* they knew it all, but there is more to running a nation than a classroom degree.

The African states that emerged at independence were not economically viable. Many countries, like Chad, Niger, and Mali, were landlocked and poor and had desertification problems; most of the inhabitants were nomads. These states relied on subsidies from France well after independence. Many suffered economic and social chaos as a result of ethnic rivalry, which weakened them further. France had eleven African colonies, and it continued to fund and provide infrastructure and manpower in strategic and technical areas.

There was still a lot of unskilled labor as the continent was just beginning to open up to a Western way of life. The new governments around Africa had been plagued with problems few years after independence.

The new leadership that emerged in the various states resorted to draconian measures in running the states, arresting and detaining opposition and all who challenged policies that were arbitrary to good governance. The new elite leaders were corrupt in many instances and were more of dictators than democrats. The new leadership all over Africa was despotic, and many independent states started off on shaky stability.

The coups in Africa started two years after independence in Sudan; by 1958, army generals took over. In 1963, Togo's president, Sylvanus Olympio, was shot dead in Lome by a group of ex–servicemen, with Sergeant Etienne Eyadema declaring the act as revenge for not being employed in the army in Togo.

However, from 1961 the armies engaged in military coups that became random events in Nigeria, Algeria, Congo, Central African Republic, etc. On January 2, 1966, Colonel Sangoule Lamizana overthrew Upper Volta's president, Maurice Yameogo, and on January 15, 1966, it was the turn of Nigeria to experience its first military coup, which swept away the discredited government of Abubakar Tafawa Balewa; it was trumped up with charges of corruption. The coups continued all over Africa until the millennium year 2000, when African states had some respite.[31]

Nigeria and all African states are bedeviled with the problems of corruption, tribalism, ethnicity, and greed. This led to bad governance

31 Ibid p. 177

and the underdevelopment of many states on the African continent who keep blaming the West for their own woes. Many African countries, however, failed to produce political and economic systems where development would flourish.

The drive for economic development led to the industrialization of many states. Various projects were set up, such as factories, steel industries, cement production companies, car assembly plants, refineries, and banks. Many of these industries required imported machines and raw materials often costing more when the goods were locally produced. This meant that importing finished goods from abroad eventually became cheaper, frustrating the whole process.

Africa's problem is that we don't have the know-how of technical skills like building machines to produce what we need. Then we cannot convert our raw materials to finished goods. We sell raw materials to Europe and America who turn them to finished products that are eventually sent back to Africa. This is our weakness, but different African states put the blame on the West for unfair trade deals.

However, oil-producing nations around Africa, like Nigeria, Gabon, Congo (Brazzaville), Algeria, and Libya, have kept afloat by the huge revenues that come from oil sales. These countries also enjoy heavy windfalls when there are conflicts in other oil-producing countries, especially in the volatile Middle East.

The first oil boom took place in 1973. With the Arab-Israeli War, crude oil prices jumped steeply from $3 to $12 in 1974. Another boom took place in 1979 when Iran and Iraq went to war. The price of oil leapt from $19 a barrel to $38. The war went on for ten years.[32]

The importing states in Africa were under a heavy strain. Togo, Benin, Ghana, Kenya, Madagascar, Senegal, Sudan, Tanzania, and Zambia all had to cut their budgets, but, despite the boom for the oil-producing states, many of them mismanaged the windfall by spending frivolously and looting the funds by awarding contracts for white-elephant projects.

These state-owned enterprises were used as conduit pipes to siphon money overseas to foreign bank accounts. It is believed that 40 percent of the whole wealth of Africa is in foreign bank accounts overseas.

Ministers preyed on government parastatals, which included the refinery, railway, and aviation industries. Many more tenders were

32 Ibid p. 276

awarded to phony companies that did not exist, and the goods never got supplied by the contractors who got paid millions of dollars, pounds, and Euros.

Private investors on the domestic and international level were discouraged and were not willing to invest, and when they did they took out all the money in form of the profits.

They sent money back overseas because the African governments were never stable, and a change in leadership could close down one's investment overnight.

The problem of electricity has traumatized many African states, and today many, including Nigeria, are big-time generator-importing nations.

The next problem faced by African states was which system of government to adopt. Many adopted capitalism, while some experimented with the communist approach, which is a socialist system of government. President Julius Nyerere of Tanzania came up with the idea of "villagisation" in 1973. It was a system whereby thousands of people would be moved within the country's population to wasteland. These were virgin fields that he expected them to turn into villages. This almost turned into a disaster.

The president had used state power to coerce people from the city, wickedly forcing them from their comfortable homes to open virgin land. It was like slavery. He moved about eleven million citizens by force, disrupting the agricultural base of the nation and bringing a shortage of one million tons in cereal maize production, almost leading the nation to famine. It was so obvious he had used military force. He silenced the press and any opposition to allow his one-party state achieve its ideological belief, which was him as president.[33]

The latest entrants are the Islamists with Sharia who are currently using violence through terrorism and religion to have their way, claiming Sharia will solve nations' problems and difficulties.

There were also other African leaders. Take, for example, Zanzibar's Abeid Karume regime, which was established after the 1964 revolution that brought an end to the ruling Arab elite. This was a clueless government.

Karume had almost no education but gained a name from being the leader of the Afro-Shirazi Party in 1963. He was also a merchant

33 Ibid p. 255-256

seaman. He deported thousands of Arabs and seized their property once he came to power. Karume knew next to nothing of how to run a country. He refused to buy drugs, even for malaria, claiming that Africans were immune to the malaria virus. He banned contraceptives. He expelled staff working with the World Health Organization. He just hoarded the funds needed to run the country despite huge foreign reserves.

There were other leaders who recklessly wasted money, like Numeiri of Sudan. He poured $11 million worth of wine into the Nile to prove the Sudan had become an Islamist nation, but by 1985, after sixteen years in power, he was overthrown in a coup.[34]

Nigeria too had been reckless with funds, especially when private businessmen brought in textile materials from overseas countries like Austria, China, and Holland. The government may have put an embargo on such imports, but when this is flouted the solution of setting the goods on fire shows low intelligence. Why not give to the homeless and poor people in the society who cannot afford clothes?

Africa's problems come from bad management, which affects the whole society at large. By the middle of the 1990s, thirty-one out of Africa's fifty-three independent states had civil unrest and were suffering from war.[35]

The wars have been between the different ethnic groups within the states. There were few between countries. Many times, the wars are fought along ethnic and religious lines, such as Christians being attacked by Islamic fanatics from the Muslim north where churches get burned down and Christians killed in thousands.

The wars in Africa have been internal battles for the political and economic control of the resources of the states. This is often triggered by ethnic and religious sentiments.

In the states where law and order had broken down, leading to chaos, the government armies and rebels have survived by looting, and defenseless civilians were the target. This has often led to an exodus of refugees fleeing to other countries for safety.[36]

The world got to know about the horrifying wars in Bosnia,

34 Ibid p. 357

35 Richard Dowden, Africa, Altered States ordinary miracles, Great Britain, Portobello Books Ltd., 2008. p. 2.

36 Ibid

Kosovo, Serbia, and Croatia. These were European countries that got international attention while those in Africa, such as Burundi and Rwanda, were believed to have been ignored for too long. Efforts at putting an end to the wars were slow.

Africa needs to help itself rather than waiting for aid from Europe and America. The backward areas need more education. The stable countries in Africa have people of higher intellect. Education has opened their eyes and broadened their minds so this has brought stability. Whenever there is crisis, lots of negotiations take place, with rare occasions when people take up arms more and more negotiations supersede bringing stability.

Many countries in Africa set up different codes of conduct, but it is always the ruling elite that break and flout the laws. The various states in Africa are grossly mismanaged financially, and this led to instability. The problem is that many leaders have been too greedy, making the basic necessities of life in any nation a Herculean task to achieve. The problems of job security and availability; heavy inflation; housing; infrastructures like well laid–out, government-planned neighborhoods that have good roads, drainage systems, electricity, and pipe-borne water have continued to elude the majority in society, thereby forming a class struggle between the haves and have-nots. This had often led to power struggle in many states, which eventually leads to the outbreak of war.

The many states in Africa have gotten a taste of this experience. Some of these states include Ethiopia, Somalia, Liberia, Sierra Leone, Congo, Burundi, Rwanda, Angola, Mozambique, Cote d'Ivoire, and Zimbabwe, where recently the white farm owners were persecuted and forced out of their farms. They had controlled the agricultural base and had sustained the economy of Zimbabwe. What has happened here is totally wrong: the taking of farmlands owned by whites who have the know-how, and then handing the property to indigenous black Zimbabweans. This is a fundamental error because they don't have the skills in certain agricultural areas. This will be discussed later.

At independence in 1960, two regions merged together to form today's Somalia. British Somalia and Italian Somalia were joined to form the Republic of Somalia. Somalia possesses a common language and a common culture based on pastoral customs and traditions. Despite extreme poverty and its lack of resources, the main energy of the Somalia government at independence was concentrated unification.

Government officials negotiated with the United States, West Germany, and Italy for military assistance and training. The USA approved 5,000 out of the requested 10,000 men. Not satisfied, they took the Soviet offer in 1963 for 10,000 army men. In 1964, Somalia and Ethiopia went to war. Victory came speedily to the Ethiopians, but, after a military coup in 1969, Soviet involvement in Somalia increased dramatically. The new Somalia leader, M. Siyad Barre, proclaimed Somalia a Marxist state. He invited the Soviets to participate in governance.

Russians took interest in Somalia for strategic reasons, with the value and plan to expand Soviet influence in the Red Sea and Indian Ocean.

In 1972, in exchange for the use of naval facilities in the northern Somalia port of Berbera, the Russians agreed to provide Somalia with increased military aid. By 1977, Somalia had acquired an army of 37,000 men with heavy artillery and a modern air force with jet fighters. Then, in the mid-1970s, the Russians switched sides. They decided to back Mengistu's Marxist regime in Ethiopia. When the Somali leader Siyad asked for Russian weapons, he was turned down. President Siyad Barre of Somalia then cancelled Somalia's treaty of friendship and cooperation with the Soviet Union and expelled all Russian personnel, but that left him without an arms supplier.

Freed from this, the Russians and Cubans committed themselves to Ethiopia on such a massive scale that the course of the wars in the Ogaden and in Eritrea changed dramatically. Facing a strike force of Cuban armor and air support, the Somalis suffered a crushing defeat in Ogaden in March 1978 and four days later announced their withdrawal.

The defeat reverberated throughout Somalia. Within weeks, officers from the Majerteyn clan of the Darod attempted to overthrow Siyad Barre. The revolt was crushed, but several leaders escaped to Ethiopia where they formed the Somali Salvation Democratic Front (SSDF) and embarked on a guerilla war against Siyad Barre's regime.

A second guerrilla war was started by the Somali National Movement (SNM), a northern group based on Isaq clans in former British Somaliland with the support of Ethiopia. Siyad reacted with harsh military and economic measures and exploited clan rivalries to keep his opponents divided. He came to rely on his own clan, the Marehan of the Darod. He gave key government positions to close family members. By 1987, it was estimated that half of the senior officer corps belonged to the marehan or related clans.

As a result of the anti-Soviet stance, Siyad was able to obtain Western support. During the 1980s the United States of America and Italy contributed sums ranging from $800 million to $1 billion in foreign aid to Somalia. Some of the money was used to pay cronies and loyalists who gave support to the government.

By 1988, Siyad Barre came to an agreement with Ethiopia under which both sides agreed to cease support for each other's opponents. The aim was for Mengistu to move troops away from the Somalia border to counter rebel advances in Eritrea and Tigray and to give Siyad an opportunity to crush the SNM in northern Somalia.

But Siyad's willingness to make deals with the old arch-enemy was seen as a gross betrayal by many Somalis; the opposition likened the pact to the Hitler-Stalin pact of 1939.

Siyad sent air force fighters and made repeated bombings raids on the city of Hargeisa, which rebels had almost captured. He sent air force fighter jets to bomb the city, killing thousands of civilians. The president did not give a damn.

The West then withdrew support. America led the way, suspending military aid in 1988 and economic aid in 1989. From then on, things were never quite the same anymore, leading to rebel competition from different groups.

A militia led by General Muhammed Farah Aideed of the United Somalia Congress (USC) controlled the south. The north was controlled by Ali Mahdi militias. That is what led to the sorry state that is Somalia today.[37]

It is unfortunate that many African states have become failed states. Somalia is among the many failed states in Africa today. Law and order has broken down for years as a result of bad leadership and mismanagement of the country's economy.

What the Islamist groups in Somalia have reverted to is the business of piracy on the high seas: taking hostages and detaining ocean vessels

37 Martin Meredith, The state of Africa, p. 464

for ransom. The government is helpless and is not in control. The rebels have taken over.

There has been no proper government in Somalia for over two decades. The country has a population of about ten million people, but over one million have fled to other countries. There are various groups perpetrating the acts of piracy, which affects passengers who travel on luxury ocean liners. It is also a menace for cargo vessels and their crew.

The Gulf of Aden and the azure waters at the foot of the Red Sea and around the Horn of Africa have become the most dangerous sea routes in the world. This is the handiwork of Somalia's pirates who keep on attacking ships.

In 2008, more than sixty vessels were captured by the pirates who often don't harm the passengers and crew but demand huge ransoms, which they have been getting. This ranges from about $1 million to about $25 million, depending on the kind of cargo. The ship owners often pass the burden to the owners of the goods who have to pay higher shipping costs.

A few remarkable incidents include a Ukraine ship carrying thirty-three tanks that was the MV Faina. The captain had died from hypertension, and some pirates also died maybe as a result of a quarrel. The ship was carrying thirty-three T-72 Russian tanks, anti-aircraft guns, and grenade launchers. The pirates demanded $20 million.

Another incident was with the Sirus Star. It was carrying a quarter of Saudi Arabia's daily output of oil; the pirates demanded $15 million. The foreign navies from the West are not able to do much because civilians are involved, and they don't want the goods damaged if they open fire.

The Gulf of Aden is host to about 10 percent of the world's shipping cargo that passes through the zone.

Somalia has become so dangerous that diplomats, journalists, and tourists have avoided the country as thousands of rootless Somali citizens fall into the hands of fundamentalist Muslims under the guise of al-Qaeda and Taliban operating in Africa.[38]

Somalia in the last ten years has had problems of drought, and whenever it rains the place floods. As a result, public service goes

---

38 The Economist, October 4th –10th , 2008, Piracy, p. 14; BBC- Focus on Africa, January–March 2009. p. 5

down and the infrastructure is in shambles. The hospitals are empty with no drugs or facilities. The warlords have been intercepting World Food Programme vessels and oftentimes stealing the funds from aid organizations. Sometimes they block the goods sent by NGOs from reaching the citizens of Somalia. The situation is so bad that aid workers have been assassinated at times.

Mogadishu is run by the Islamic Courts Union, which is built on the Sharia court system. The instability has brought about refugee problems where people travel to foreign countries and become illegal immigrants.[39]

Sierra Leone

Sierra Leone followed the path to ruin with the conflict that arose between the Creoles and indigenous chiefs in the state. The Creoles were the mixed–race people who were half European and half African. They were the offspring of the early white settlers who had relationships or married Africans at the time.

Sierra Leone has experienced a lot of coups and counter coups like many of the Africa states. In 1978, Siaka Stevens emerged as a leader in the country. He ran a one-party state and within twenty months had ruined the economy of Sierra Leone, which never fully recovered.

The country is blessed with the best diamonds in the universe, but, despite the wealth generated from the diamonds and the huge revenues that accrued to the state, the money has gone into private pockets. The diamond trade is very lucrative, and the diamonds are easily stolen and easy to find. Many people succeed in smuggling and selling them overseas as diamonds sell anywhere in the world. The diamond was once the mainstay of Sierra Leone's economy and provided the bulk of the government's revenue.

However, corruption, the major problem in Africa, as well as lawlessness and mismanagement, led to the illegal mining of the mineral. Gradually theft, illegal digging, and prospecting led to smuggling and the astronomical levels of corruption left the state government with almost nothing.

The Lebanese were encouraged to settle in Sierra Leone during the time of British rule with a view to boosting trade and strengthening

39 Newsweek, July 31st, 2006, p. 44. Africa's Taliban by Rod Nordland.

the economy. They traded and milked the country dry, leaving Sierra Leone at the mercy of foreign aid. The locations where the diamonds are found are often turned from peaceful settlements to boisterous, noisy areas where prospectors and miners of all shade and color dig the ground looking frantically for the precious mineral.

Raw diamonds look like broken pieces of Coca-Cola bottles. If found, a man slips one in his mouth. If anybody is aware he has it, his life is in danger.

African countries are cursed by their minerals, which they cannot manage properly. Countries like Angola, Sierra Leone, Congo, and the Central African Republic are cursed as diamonds have brought them pain through conflicts and war.

South Africa, Namibia, and Botswana have more government regulation and activity on mining and have utilized the revenues generated in the proper development of their states.

But in the African-controlled regions, it has created wars and poverty. The British-based South African company De Beers has controlled the diamond trade for decades. The coups continued to destabilize Sierra Leone, and by 1992 General Momoh was overthrown by Valentine Strasser. The government ended the same way: with greed and corruption undermining and destroying the regime.[40]

The Revolutionary United Front (RUF) began as a kind of Marxist movement led by students from Fourah Bay College. But once they joined the guerrilla fighters, they lost control of the RUF to Foday Sankoh, who was being financed at the time by Charles Taylor of Liberia.

Foday Sankoh was a photographer in the army, and he turned the RUF into a terror organization. He compelled the members of the group to use hard drugs like brown-brown and cocaine. It was a mixture of cocaine and gun powder.

He kidnapped children and turned them into child soldiers making them kill their parents if he took them from their homes and also making them rape relatives. These horrific acts traumatized the kids, but they could never run away as there was nowhere to go back to. The RUF became their families. They were noted for murder, rape, and cutting off hands and feet. The unlucky victims were told that with no

40 Africa, Altered States Ordinary Miracles, page 293.

hands, they could not vote in an election. This was the opposition group acting as guerrillas fighting the Sierra Leonean government.

However, in 1996 Strasser was ousted in a coup, and the British government offered him exile in England, but he was eventually murdered. Julius Maada Bio took over and he was encouraged to conduct elections. Ahmed Tejan Kabbah, a lawyer and former civil servant, emerged as president of Sierra Leone. He signed a peace agreement with the RUF. This, however, did not work, and he was overthrown within one year by Paul Koroma.

Nigeria had used its initiative to convince other ECOWAS member states to send peace-keeping forces to Sierra Leone. They fought their way into Freetown and restored Tejan Kabbah to power.

The RUF regrouped, but the Nigerian troops defeated them with about 3,000 people killed. The war ended. The wars and conflict in Africa have been a battle for the resources, not tribalism or anything else as we are made to believe.

The wars in Sierra Leone lasted a decade. The rebels were backed by Liberia's former president Charles Taylor, who is currently facing war crimes charges at The Hague. The citizens of this country had their body parts cut off, leading to the many amputees that can be seen in the society today. They are the physical signs left after the war. The affected are called the "cut men" since they have no money. Society abandoned them. Buses drive by and don't stop to pick them up. They are known as the "forgotten victims" of the war. The notorious rebel nicknamed C.O. Cut Hands, which means *commanding officer cuts hands*, was responsible for the dastard acts of maiming those who refused to abide with his demands.[41] The diamonds used to finance the conflict were eventually called blood diamonds, and people were asked not to buy or patronize the diamonds coming from those states during the conflicts.

In the first two decades of independence, there were forty successful coups and countless attempted coups in Africa—many were bloodless. By 1979, Nigeria had become the world's sixth largest oil producer with revenues soaring to $24 billion a year. Such riches, however, set off a vicious scramble for political office and the wealth that went

41 BBC Focus on Africa, page 28, July–September 2006, by Ofeibea Quist-Arcton. P. 28

with it. Access to the government spending process was the gateway to fortune.

Blood Diamonds: Liberia and Sierra Leone

The United States had set up the Republic of Liberia in 1847. America sent three hundred black families, after the end of slavery in America, to Liberia in Africa. The new state already had indigenous Africans who were looked down on by the American settlers who were also black, but descendents of slaves.

The Liberians were called Americo-Liberians and behaved like colonial masters. When colonial rule came to an end in West Africa in the 1960s, the Liberian system continued its colonial system of management. It was run like an oligarch of a few ruling elites, and they were proud of their American heritage.

The country was run by the prominent families that emerged: the Barclays, the Tubmans, the Kings, and the Tolberts. By the 1970s, William Tolbert emerged as president. He brought few reforms from the old order but began to amass personal wealth. He brought in family members to serve as ministers, ambassadors, and personal aides. The economic mainstay came from the rubber plantations, with Firestone producing tires in Liberia for the huge American market. Iron was another product mined and developed, which brought in 50 percent of the country's revenues. The disparity between the ruling elite and the public was too far when it came to economic wealth, which eventually brought demonstrations.

President Tolbert had increased the price of rice by 50 percent. It was hoped it would encourage local production, but where importation was favored it was seen as a means to enrich the Tolbert family.

President William Tolbert had ordered the police and army to shoot demonstrators, which led to huge crisis and discontent.[42]

By 1980, on the twelfth of April, twenty-eight-year-old Master Sergeant Samuel Doe overthrew the government in a bloody coup, killing the president and all top serving ministers.

Samuel Doe did no better. He had used ethnicity by promoting his tribesmen, the Krahn, who were minorities out of Liberia's sixteen ethnic groups. He used an iron hand to rule and loot state corporations like the

42 Gunther John, Inside Africa, p. 827.

petroleum refining company, the marketing produce corporations, and the logging corporations. Along with cronies, they milked the country dry, bringing Liberia to its knees.

The American government continued to fund and support Liberia, despite the despot who ruled the country, because the American embassy in Monrovia served as an information network to monitor activities around Africa. The United States of America had set up the Robertsfield airport base during the Second World War. It was used for landing and refueling US military planes.

Samuel Doe banned all political activity. He felt threatened by the educated opposition, being almost a stark illiterate who learnt the basics from the streets before joining the army. He survived counter coups but finally fell.

The United States had continued to support his government because he protected America's interest and also because the United States government did not know how bad things had turned out to be.

By the ninth of September, 1990, Samuel Doe was killed in the most gruesome manner, which was recorded and televised around the world. His ears were cut off and he was made to eat them by Field Marshal Prince Yomi Johnson. Amos Sawyer, a university professor, became head of the new interim government of national unity. He only controlled some parts of Liberia as other areas were held by rebels.

Eventually Charles Taylor became the president after an election in July 1997 through Taylor's National Patriotic Party (NPP).

Charles Taylor's ambition, however, was not confined to Liberia. He set his sight on neighboring Sierra Leone whose government had provided the ECOMOG forces of Nigeria with a base at Lungi airport just north of the capital Freetown.

What attracted Taylor to Sierra Leone were the rich alluvial diamond fields of Kono, less than a hundred miles from Liberia's border.[43]

In the mid-1990s, the African continent was plagued with war and more than half of the fifty-three African countries were experiencing civil disturbances and civil war.

The irony was that people died not from gunfire, but as a result of bad water, hunger, and disease.

The wars were often times caused by internal conflicts triggered by

---

43 Martin Meredith, The state of Africa. p. 545

battles for power, often called power tussle for the control and wealth within states usually among the different ethnic groups.

The world got to know about Bosnia, Croatia, Serbia, and Kosovo because they were engulfed by war. Nigeria is chaos, but the chaos is created, organized by the government. Chaos allows it to stay in power.

Africans are gun-toting, mindless warriors or hopeless, helpless victims who can do nothing for themselves, doomed to endless poverty, violence, and hunger. Only foreign aid and foreign aid workers can save them. The endless images of guns, oppression, hunger, and disease create the impression that this is all that ever happens in Africa.

Congo

The Democratic Republic of Congo became independent on the thirtieth of June, 1960. It had started wrongly with the new elite group that emerged. The president, Patrice Lumumba, had nothing good to say of the European powers and immediately started to dismantle the structures they had set up to govern the state. It did not take long before he got killed.

The Congo had been different from other African states because it was the personal property of King Leopold II. In 1885, he got international approval recognizing the Congo as his property. It has a very large area believed to be a million square miles. It possesses minerals like copper, uranium, cobalt, and diamonds.

By 1959, Congo supplied the global village with 10 percent of its copper, 50 percent of the cobalt, and 70 percent of the world's diamonds. The Belgians kept the Congo away from outside influence, almost isolating it completely.

This stifled the emergence of an elite group. They had prevented the indigenous people from education, which kept them backward. It was only in 1950 they allowed a few of the black indigenes to begin the secondary school education.

Mobutu Sese Seko took over with the support of the United States, Canada, France, and Belgium, who all needed Congo for the minerals and raw materials within the nation.

In 1968, Uganda's military, led by the army chief Idi Amin Dada, succeeded in smuggling gold out of the Congo. The Congo was just too large a country with porous borders and many uninhabited areas.

By 1971, Idi Amin organized a coup and successfully overthrew the Ugandan president Milton Obote. Once the neighboring states got to hear about Congo's porous borders, they took advantage and started looting the country's minerals. Zimbabwean army generals joined in the lucrative looting of Congo's minerals. Uganda also looted timber from Congo.

Rwanda also got involved in mining columbite and tantalite, used in mobile phones and computers, from Congo. Even UN peacekeepers have been found to barter, trading UN weapons for minerals like gold with rebel groups they are supposed to disarm.

However, in the early 1990s Rwanda exploded in an ethnic war that affected Congo and Zaire. Rwandan Tutsis, who had left their country during the Hutu uprising in 1959, which went on for two decades and resulted in the terrible genocide in 1994, made their return from exile in Uganda and invaded Rwanda. The years of mobilization had gotten to the peak and all who had gone in exile seeking asylum in Uganda, Tanzania, Burundi, and Zaire returned with a menace to Rwanda with the backing of Yoweri Kaguta Museveni, the president of Uganda. He gave them weapons. Mobutu had, on the other hand, tried to help Rwanda by sending troops to rout the Tutsis, but this effort failed.

By 1994, Kigali in Rwanda fell to the invading troops. The government of the extremist Hutu militia, the Interahamwe, fled into exile. The Interahamwe executed over a million Tutsis and liberal and moderate Hutus who they saw as supporters of the Tutsis. Civilians were used as human shields in the war.

Paul Kegame emerged as the new leader, and he invaded the Congo for supporting the Hutu government, bringing an end to Mobutu's government. Mobutu fled and later died in Morocco. This brought back over two million people who had been in exile in Congo.

The Rwandans helped install Laurent Desire Kabila on seventeenth of May, 1997. At his inauguration, Kabila was widely hailed as representing a new dawn in Congo. It did not take time for his leadership to crumble. He had no political program or strategic plan or vision. He did not know how to run the government or a country. He relied on Rwanda. It was the same old stories: putting discordant voices in detention and prison, which included the media and journalists. There were a lot of Rwandans in his cabinet and Rwandan troops were controlling the streets in Congo. The Congolese saw him as a puppet of Rwanda.

He began to distance himself from the Rwandans and Banyamulenge who had helped install him as president. The militias continued to operate from Congo despite the new government in place. Rwanda and Uganda were attacked by dissidents from within the Congo to the annoyance of the leaders of these two countries, Museveni and Kegame. They planned regime change for Laurent Kabila.

Laurent Kabila was a small-time militant. He had forgotten who installed him as president. Rwanda had all the Congolese army in their support, and it did not take long before Kabila was deserted. The hydroelectric plant supplying electricity to Kinshasa and other parts of Congo was seized.

Kabila retaliated by encouraging the killing of Tutsis, Kegame's tribesmen who were currently in charge of Rwanda, through Congo's state radio stations where they encouraged the public to pick up machetes, spears, arrows, spades, electric irons, and any other weapon they could use to kill the Tutsis. And they did kill them.

However it was Angola and Zimbabwe that saved Kabila from regime change. Rwanda and Uganda did not succeed in regime change, but they got control of the northeast of Congo's territory.

The neighboring countries took charge and control of the minerals in Congo. Zimbabwe and Angola handled diamond and petroleum while Rwanda and Uganda controlled the eastern Congo. They also controlled the trade there. Consumer goods were brought in by aircraft, which also included food stuffs, and they departed with gold, coltan, and diamonds. The plunder continued, and the citizens were poor and divided. And then a big quarrel started between the plunderers, Uganda and Rwanda. It was the UN Security Council that demanded Rwanda and Uganda withdraw from the Congo immediately.

All these wars brought about the blood diamond issue where diamonds and other minerals like coltan were said to be used to finance these wars, also bringing about the slogan "no blood on my satellite" because coltan is used to make electronics like satellites and telephones, etc. Kabila continued to mismanage and misrule the Congo, and by the sixteenth of January, 2001, he was assassinated by one of his security guards. It seemed like a palace coup plot, but eventually his son was given the mandate of his father to continue as the new president.[44]

Zimbabwe, on the other hand, had become independent in 1980, one of the last countries in Africa to gain independence from the colonists. Robert Mugabe emerged as the president of a fabulous African nation. The country was well run and organized, and the economy was aligned to the Western countries. The agricultural sectors were controlled by the white European farmers, and most were in control of the fertile land.

The Europeans who had settled for decades in Zimbabwe also controlled the manufacturing and mining sectors. That was why the country worked and prospered. Zimbabwe was called Rhodesia under the Ian Smith government, but at independence the name changed in 1980.

The Ian Smith government had gotten independence from Britain on November 11, 1965, and was in control until 1980 when power was given to black indigenous Africans.

President Robert Mugabe started off nicely, even appointing white Europeans into the new government as ministers, and ran the system democratically, but a decade later things turned around.

He wanted to take back the agricultural lands the Europeans had controlled and invested their whole lives in. It was the beginning of the wrong decisions that led to failed African states.[45]

Robert Mugabe wanted the British government to pay compensation for the land controlled by the Europeans. The whole idea sprang into his mind when in the late 1980s and very early 1990s Chief MKO Abiola of Nigeria, the millionaire tycoon and ITT Africa and Asia boss, also known to have funded the nationalist cause in Zimbabwe and South Africa, had triggered the call for reparation in Africa. He asked foreign governments in the West to pay for slavery and colonization by compensating Africans with several billions for what he described as a wrong.

Tony Blair, the British prime minister at the time, did not buy the idea and rather discussed that Zimbabwe should concern itself with

---

44 Kassim Kayira, BBC Focus on Africa, July–September 2006, p. 10–12.

45 New African summer 2007, Zimbabwe Special Edition: "Our Cause Is Africa's Cause."

good governance, human rights, and the rule of law. Robert Mugabe then took to draconian laws where he took the land from the white settlers. He seized the lands used for the state's agricultural survival from the white farmers and handed it over to incompetent black farmers who could not manage or run the farms. The black farmers didn't know how to run certain agricultural systems. They knew nothing of subsistence farming let alone operating and running the sophisticated irrigation systems and management of the complex business of running a farm.

They ripped up irrigation pipes and sold them as scrap metal, dams that needed maintenance were allowed to collapse, and this collapsed the economy.

The British government then imposed sanctions to pressure President Mugabe, but he refused to change. The Nigerian government then invited the white farmers to Nigeria. Some took the initiative and relocated to the state of Kwara. The sanctions were targeted at Mugabe, but they affected the whole country. Britain influenced other countries and they complied because Mugabe had been in office for almost three decades, turning the country into his personal property.

The sanctions took their toll because many found Mugabe guilty. First, he had overstayed as a democratically elected president, and then he did not do changes the right way. Petroleum products were intercepted carrying fuel destined for Zimbabwe. They offered higher prices for the product to get it diverted, leading to fuel shortage and queues. They imposed a ban on spare parts. This led to an industrial paralysis as spare parts are needed to run factories and mines. The financial institutions like the World Bank and IMF refused to give balance of payment support and Zimbabwe got no loans. This put a hold on investors, making them tread carefully for the safety of their funds.

The Americans also tried to reach him, but he continued with his anti-Western stance, which brought about the politics of regime change in 2004. The American president, through the secretary of state at the time, announced the United States' and European Union's withdrawal from assisting Zimbabwe. It was because of his authoritarian rule, draconian policies, and cynical land reform policies, which Collin Powell alleged had rendered millions hungry.

The entire Zimbabwean economy was near collapse; reckless

and monumental corruption produced inflation of 300 percent and unemployment rose to about 70 percent. This also brought shortages of fuel and other basic necessities.

Many critics often say that from history, the United States of America has not cared about other people, let alone Africans. That is not true. Bad governance affects all countries of the world, especially European countries and America. This is because war-torn countries round the world have the privilege and elite class heading to Europe and America as illegal immigrants and refugees. It is always these countries that accommodate displaced people. It is the reason for the interference in the domestic matters of these countries by the West.

The world has become a global village with the introduction of news reporters and journalists now able to bring the happenings around the world into our homes via satellite. The wars are seen on our screens so the world powers take interest in events around the world. In the past, you only found it reported in the newspapers or on the radio or television, but now you actually see the direct happenings in your living rooms. As a result, people cringe and the world powers have to intervene, sometimes breaking international law.

Sanctions have effects because they could bring the economy of a nation to its knees and create social challenges that cause disaffection for the possibility of regime change. This also can be done by the opposition parties calling on Western countries to intervene through sanctions. The Movement for Democratic Change headed by Morgan Tsvangirai went all out on March 29, 2003, to lobby Western countries to sanction Zimbabwe. His call also embraced NGOs, which had to join in putting pressure on Mugabe.

The sanctions would have been very effective if the African Union had taken a stand in joining the West. But Thabo Mbeki, who was then the president of South Africa, was just too kind and gentle; he would not want to hurt a friend. He saved Zimbabwe. South Africa has been a strategic and powerful ally to Zimbabwe as it allowed Zimbabwe to get electricity from its national grid despite a huge annual debt of $2.6 billion. South Africa also controlled Zimbabwe's trade routes, making Zimbabwe dependent on South Africa.

Zimbabwe has become the symbol of leadership failure. A leader who stayed in power for thirty years should not be encouraged to continue, especially at the age of eighty-six-years-old. He had effectively stolen the destiny of other citizens who might have served the country better.

The press in the society has been silenced, and political opponents have been terrorized. They fled forever, not looking back. About 3.4 million Zimbabweans, a quarter of the population, have left the country and moved abroad. It is believed one million are in England alone. The population figures quoted are true because the central bank, through Western Union remittances, has the figures.

Expatriate Zimbabweans send funds to the tune of between $1 million and $3 million daily from overseas. If the Western nations shut their doors, what would happen? People have to think deeply before they start blaming Europe and America for the slightest and flimsiest excuses.

The African neighbors of Zimbabwe are not happy with the constant crowd of desperate migrants. Every Thursday, South Africa deports thousands of Zimbabweans caught without work permits or valid immigration papers. Still, more than a million have melded into the population. Botswana is making newer extensions to the countries' border fence. How can we continue to blame the West for our own bad leadership problems?

If the West will not buy the raw materials and minerals, it's another problem since we cannot develop the raw materials to finish products. Many nations cannot even mine or locate any minerals in their states or nations without foreign help. It is time to reinvent Africa.[46]

46 Newsweek, March 1, 2004, p. 42.

Chapter Four

Nigeria the Sleeping Giant

Nigeria is an independent country found within the African region. It is one of the fifty-three independent states of Africa. It is located in West Africa along the coastal regions, and Lagos State, which was the capital, had been the arrival point of the British who annexed it in 1862.

Then in 1914 Lord Lugard merged the north and south together, bringing about a very complex twist that has caused the friction between the states of the north and south, triggered by religious, ethnic, and tribal differences.

The country is divided into three regions—the northern, eastern, and western region—and remains so to date. But technically it is five regions, if you include the Niger Delta and middle belt regions. There are thirty-six states in Nigeria today. Nigeria has an estimated population of 140 million people, making it the largest on the continent in terms of manpower.

Nigeria became independent in 1960. It turned fifty years old on October 1, 2010. The independence had been offered on a platter of gold. There are a bewildering variety of people and languages, but the three major languages that dominate are the Hausa, Igbo, and Yoruba, with English as the official language of the nation.

The lack of homogeneity of Nigeria is beyond doubt. Its overriding political and national problem is the curse of the great nation, which remains sectionalism, ethnicity, religious intolerance, and massive corruption. The country is still slow to industrialize.

Another disappointment is the unpatriotic and corrupt attitudinal thinking of the political class that rules Nigeria. The political thinking is wrong in the nation and has aggravated the poverty in the nation. The political class believes everything is money. They compete in the game of acquisition of wealth. The Nigerian nation, just like its other sister states that form the African Union, had gotten its independence too early and without much experience, except those with Western education. They brought on the idea of the nationalist movement toward getting a free and independent nation from the colonial masters who were seen as parasites.

The amalgamation of the north and south in 1914 had been a marriage of convenience where the three main groups were forced to live together in harmony. But many times there were discordant tunes, most of the time emerging from the north with its religious conflicts from the Muslims who oftentimes provoked the other groups by their wanton killing of Christians and burning of churches. This often led to reprisal attacks in other regions on the northerners.

But no matter the challenges of nationhood, full-scale war has not been an option to toy with anymore. There are intermarriages within all the ethnic groups and heavy investments in business to engage in warfare like the ones in Rwanda and Liberia.

The Nigerian elite and cream of the society have ethnic considerations as the least thought on their minds, and when they meet to mingle they talk big deals. The Nigerian elite have always known how to close ranks and have taken care of themselves across the country's ethnic borders. Whatever happens at the top of the political parties, the ruling class survives. The top professionals in the political class, business, academia, the military, and traditional rulers, are tied together, forming strings of connections in a grand alliance to continue to dominate the upper reaches of the Nigerian economy.

However many people had expected it to have collapsed and disintegrated years ago and have described it as one of the failed states in Africa that actually works. It is still a mystery. The secret lies in the layers of networks that come with extended family networks, personal ties, school fraternities, church connections, and scores of others.

The hidden wiring also creates the presidents, makes fortunes, and prevents wars. But it also ensures the majority are kept outside the ruling elite-owner circle.

The mystery that keeps Nigeria going is unknown to many. Nigeria is a religious state, and continued prayers help avert many of the calamities that come its way. The enemies of Nigeria keep trying to destabilize it.

The first of October, 2010, marked the fiftieth anniversary of independence. Two bombs were detonated, killing innocent people at the Eagle Square at Abuja. The militant group Mend claimed responsibility.

Also, rocket launchers and bombs, including anti-aircraft missiles, were smuggled in thirteen different containers into Nigeria from Iran. They were brought in to destabilize the government of President Goodluck Jonathan.

The enemies of Nigeria keep on trying all sorts of things, but the vigilant security operatives get them exposed, frustrating their efforts to destabilize the nation.

The nation of Nigeria experienced the unbelievable on December 25, 2009, Christmas Day. A twenty-three-year-old Nigerian from the northern region, identified as Abdul Farouk Umar Abdul Mutallab, believed to be the son of a former bank chairman, the First Bank of Nigeria's Umaru Mutallab, had been arrested by security operatives in the United States over activities of terrorism. He had tried to detonate a bomb planted in his underwear aboard a Northwest flight from Amsterdam to Detroit, Michigan, in the United States of America. This brought Nigeria shock and shame. That was the first suicide bomber produced by the Islamic fundamentalist groups who was a Nigerian citizen. America responded by putting Nigeria on the terror list, which is a ranking where a country is classified as high security risk.[47]

The problem of Nigeria is the absence of good leadership coupled with massive corruption, but otherwise Nigeria is a wonderful country.

The problem of corruption has eaten so deeply into the fabric of society that it affects everything. The power problem, electricity, is made worse deliberately by saboteurs in the system, associates of the generator and fuel cartel. Many times the electricity has no problems—

---

47 Sunday Independent, December 27 2009 and The Punch January 8, 2010

they just switch off so that the generator sales can improve and the daily consumption of fuel petrol and diesel can increase.

The former president spent $16 billion, an amount that can electrify the whole nation, which is just the size of three of the largest American states put together. But there was no improvement. Nobody sincerely questioned where all the money went. In 2007, the country had about $60 billion in its reserves, but after three years it is merely $20 billion. The high revenues from the oil flush over a decade cannot be accounted for, as the infrastructures in the nation are down. The roads are worse than when the military ruled the nation. It seems the military managed the country better than the civilians on many fronts.

The ruling party in Nigeria has failed to understand that the PDP is the driver of the nation and is not the nation itself. In other words, the PDP feel that they are the Nigerian nation rather than its representatives. This means that every decision taken by the PDP leadership is viewed as being good for the country without consulting the wider nation. So many ethnic groups make democracy building difficult, but not impossible.

The power-sharing formula might be good but might not bring the best out to govern the country. Take for instance if, in the period of rotational presidency, the slot is given to the north of Nigeria. The best candidate might be in the east or southern part of Nigeria. This system will deprive the nation of the best and most effective leader at the time. The system continues to divide the country and flares tribal and ethnic sentiments.

Nigeria cannot be divided into the north and south. There are three zones in the south of Nigeria: the southwest, with the Yoruba tribes; the eastern part with the Ibos, who call themselves Biafrans; and the Niger Delta region, which is the south region that produces the oil. The other is the northern part of Nigeria where you have the Hausa and Fulani groups, and then you have the middle belt region of Nigeria, Benue area, and the plateau state where you have Jos. These middle belt areas are not inhabited by Hausas but by other groups: the Igalas, Idomas, etc. Free and fair elections that produce the best candidates with the highest numbers of votes is what works in a real democracy.

It can be widely acknowledged from the experiences of countries like China who are gradually embracing democracy that a poor, rapidly developing nation often does best with a benevolent dictator.

Democracies, and particularly messy coalition democracies, are ineffective in imposing some kind of discipline and sacrifices that bootstrapping economies require. Nigeria as a nation has continued to grow steadily. Despite the huge population, it has managed to control any volatile uprising.

The Boko Haram Islamic group is similar to insurgent groups like al-Qaeda and Taliban but on a milder scale. They are also influenced from the Middle East with cash inducements. The introduction of Sharia during the administration of former president Olusegun Obasanjo, between 1999 and 2007, had come from Zamfara state, one of Nigeria's northern states.

The governor, Ahmed Sanni Yerima, was very clever. He used to be clean shaven like a cadet officer, but, enticed by the funds coming from the Middle East (Saudi Arabia, Iran, etc.) urging Muslims to adopt the radical side of Islam, which promoted jihad and Sharia, he jumped on the band wagon. The enticement of millions of dollars tickled his fancy: free money that nobody would question. He immediately grew his beard wild and bushy and introduced Sharia up north. He decided to ban alcohol, he changed the dress code, and he said men and women could not go on the same bus or ride on a motorcycle together. He declared Sharia as the state law, nullifying the constitution in his state.

He tried to declare an Islamic state and got away with it. He introduced the Sharia legal code that included stoning for adultery and armed robbery and cutting of hands for theft. He did cut off a man's hand for stealing a goat to show his seriousness. The other northern governors hailed him, not understanding the implication of this new radical idea.

They supported him because all that has happened since independence is north versus south, and since the presidency was with a southerner they disdained him. They all went along with Sharia, causing tension and uproar around Nigeria and the world.

This became the issue for almost three years, diverting attention away from other crucial matters concerning the proper governance of Nigeria. The northerners had ruled Nigeria for about thirty-five years, and certain elite groups had become accustomed to believing it was a right for the north to produce the presidency all the time.

The irony was that the man whose hand was cut off to show seriousness was rehabilitated by the governor himself. People saw him controlling a lucrative warehouse where commodities were being sold. This was reported in some newspapers with the picture taken. I think his name was Jengadi.

The governor got his funding, and, since it was heard all over the world, he was seen to have complied with the demand to introduce Sharia and bring in the theocratic system of government being practiced in Iran. He had to show that the money was well spent for that purpose and nobody could have accused him of taking money without performing the task. The governor, however, got into the news recently by marrying a twelve-year-old Egyptian girl, causing uproar in Nigeria with NGOs and women rights organizations condemning him as a pedophile. Child rights activists caused a scandal of the affair in the media, but he said Islam allows child marriages.

The other bad events are the kidnapping of people for ransom. This has continued with hostages also taken from oil platforms in the Niger Delta region for weeks, with the abductors asking for huge sums of money for their release.

These are some of the problems Nigeria faces as a nation. But, despite these failings, the Nigerian state continues to exist. The ruling elite find the arrangement okay because it brings surprises. Nigeria is a place where, with luck, your fortunes can change overnight.

Chapter Five

Internal Conflicts, Genocide, Refugee Problems, and Theocratic Regimes

After the First World War ended in 1918, many of the world powers and countries around the globe realized the evil effects and consequences of fighting a war. The major leaders then formed the League of Nations, which had its headquarters in Geneva. They also set up an international court where disputes between nations could be settled amicably in a peaceful manner.

The League of Nations, however, had its shortcomings as it failed to prevent another outbreak of war: the Second World War. Germany triggered the war by asking for its seized colonies in Africa that the League of Nations confiscated after the First World War.

"Hitler's war" was started in 1939 and ended 1945. It was devastating. Millions of people were killed and many towns turned to rubble.[48]

After the cessation of hostilities, the world powers—the United States of America, the United Kingdom, France, Russia, and China—called a meeting with fifty other nations in San Francisco, a city in America.

The outcome of the meeting resulted in the formation of the United Nations. The charter of the organization was drawn up and signed by

48 Wiki Answers, "What Were the Causes of World War 2," http://wiki.answers.com/Q/what were the causes of world war. p. 2

all nations present. The main content of the charter was the agreement between all nations that there must be peace and security throughout the world.

Secondly, disputes between nations must be settled amicably, and all other nations should see that conflicts are resolved without resorting to violent wars.

The main organs of the United Nations include these:

1. The General Assembly;
2. The Security Council;
3. The Economic and Social Council;
4. The Trusteeship Council;
5. The Secretariat; and the
6. International Court of Justice.

There are number of specialized agencies working with the United Nations. The World Health Organization (WHO), which has staffs working in many countries throughout the world, finds solutions to the various diseases around the globe.

The Food and Agricultural Organization (FAO) is an organ of the United Nation that works in poor countries and finds ways to improve food production. The World Bank gives loans to countries in need for the various infrastructural developments they might need to embark on.

The Trusteeship Council was set up by the United Nations after the Second World War ended in 1945. During the First World War, Germany had instigated the war and was defeated. The penalties cost the Germans the loss of their African colonies, which were taken over by the League of Nations. Each of these colonies taken over was administered by nations who were members of the League of Nations. The colonies were called *the mandated territories* and were put under the supervision of Trusteeship Council. The colonies later became trust territories, which were supervised by Trusteeship Council on matters relating to education, social, economic, and political development of these territories. The council was to prepare them for autonomy, which eventually led to their being independent states.

The International Court of Justice has its seat at The Hague. Judges selected are those with high moral character with the highest judicial qualification. All member nations are expected to comply with the decision of the court, but if parties refuse to abide with a decision of the court, the case may be referred to the Security Council.[49]

The court is in permanent session except during judicial vacations. It has the ability to hear cases anywhere in the world besides The Hague. The court is a forum for settling international disputes between countries.

The United Nations also responds to natural disasters like the Indian Ocean tsunami, which had a devastating effect. The United Nations spearheaded the largest humanitarian operation the region has ever seen. This brought international aid workers, survivors, and soldiers, including the navy who worked side by side to deliver food and medical supplies donated by Western and Asian countries.

The United Nation also has other agencies like UNICEF, which assists, UNHCR, which assists and protects refugees, the World Food Programme, and the World Health Organization. All have been involved in various activities where international conflict and disasters have been going on for almost seven decades.

The United Nations as an intergovernmental body has clout among its member states; only the United Nations could convince the Singaporean government and negotiate with them the plight of the refugees rescued at sea. It was on the recognition of the body that the refugees were allowed to land in Singapore. The government had said as long as it was the United Nations handling the refugees' camp and standing as guarantor, it would open its doors. The UN has the ability to persuade immigration officials of a dozen foreign countries to admit refugees and resolve problem cases.

The United Nations enjoys the support of many governments because it does not belong to anyone. However, when national issues flare up between states, the United Nations is preferred because it is seen as an embodiment of collective interest. The United Nations is

49 Lawal O.A. 'O' Level Government of West Africa, Ibadan Educational books (Nigeria) Ltd., Heinemann Educational Books, 1982. P. 218

recognized and unchallenged as the coordinating authority, which gives its collective actions and decisions legitimacy and recognition.[50]

The United Nations is a highly respected organization and countries contact it before embarking on international issues that could breach the peace and security around the globe. Even the only superpower, which is the United States of America, had to inform the United Nations about its concerns in Iraq, Sudan, and even Haiti.

The United Nations, despite many of its successes and strengths, has its weakness. The permanent members have to agree with any major decision.

The American invasion of Iraq was not agreed to by all members. This meant the United States should not have invaded Iraq, but President Bush ignored the veto from some members and went into Iraq unilaterally. He also rejected United Nations participation, humiliating allies who felt threatened by this new posture that was contrary to the rules of the United Nations.

The United Nations has also been unable to reduce the arms race for weapons among various countries, now especially with the nuclear threat from such combustible regions in the Middle East like Iran and North Korea, which the Bush administration described as "the axis of evil."

The year 1974 created a new global structure where President Richard Nixon and the secretary of state, Henry Kissinger, created the nuclear Non-Proliferation Treaty (NPT) where countries who wanted to buy nuclear reactors and fuel had to sign the document promising never to build a bomb, with an additional agreement to open their nuclear sites to inspection. They wanted a situation where it would be difficult for countries to turn civilian technology, which could include producing electricity, into the use of nuclear weapons. India had bought a reactor that year from Canada for civilian purposes and experimented making plutonium. Its scientists secretly shaped the metal into a bomb and exploded it. India declared it a peaceful nuclear test. But the cat was out of the bag. The countries that signed the treaty were 183, but Iran and North Korea cheated and disobeyed, which made them outlaws.[51]

---

50 Shashi Tharoor, Newsweek, January 31st, 2005, p. 17.

51 Joseph Cirincione, Newsweek, December 2008-February 2009, Bush's very dangerous deal, p. 31.

However, despite the efforts of the United Nations as an organization that helps to keep the peace globally, political conflict still occurs today regularly. Most times they are conflicts within states; many are domestic conflicts caused by the struggle for power and economic resources within a country along ethnic lines. The wars have also been as a result of border disputes or groups and ethnic nationalities wanting to secede from an old union of merged states. It could also spring from religious conflicts between Muslims and Christians or bigger nations trying to annex smaller ones: Libya and Chad, Iraq and Kuwait.

The wars in Serbia (Kosovo), Russia (Chechnya), China (Tibet), Iran, Iraq, Vietnam, and African states like Rwanda, Burundi, Sudan, Darfur, Liberia, and Sierra Leone, had devastating effects on the society and populations of these nations.

The political conflicts come with consequences, such as genocide, which are acts committed with intent to destroy, in whole or in part, a national, ethnic, racial, or religious group, including causing of serious bodily harm or mental harm, preventing births, or inflicting conditions calculated to lead to a group's destruction.[52]

These conflicts trigger mass movement of people who become devastated and in trying to escape from harm's way become refugees who many times end up as the illegal immigrants around the world.

The year 1979 was labeled the year of refugees, but 1980 even proved worse, and by 1981 it seemed to have arrived with a grim promise of yet another season of displacements.

Today we have more than thirty-two million refugees around the world, and refugee problems are treated as an aberration of world politics: self-contained, disconnected, sporadic, and unpredictable, roughly comparable to natural disasters. In Iraq, over two million fled the country and refused to return. Only about 5 percent have returned. But in Afghanistan and Kosovo millions of refugees came back to their home state. The American government had engineered not only regime change but total dismantling of the state.

The 1980, 1990s, and the millennium years continue to witness huge populations of displaced people who are fleeing from troubled zones, either as a result of war or economic prosperity searching for a better future in more prosperous and stable societies. These have

---

52 The Economist, July 31st, 2004, p. 33,

resulted from the ancient themes of human greed, betrayal of popular will, lust for power, and ethnic hatred.

The prevention of the refugee problem escalating to great heights will be the capacity to maintain global stability. This can only be possible by peacefully resolving disputes and ameliorating the economic preconditions of violence on a long-term prospect.

Who is a refugee? The United Nations recognizes three categories of people: stateless people, those who have been stripped of their citizenship while abroad or upon being sent into exile. The late singer Mariam Makeba falls in the former category where she was branded by the South African government under apartheid regime as a political singer. When she addressed the United Nations summit in 1963, the South African government cancelled her passport and revoked her citizenship. It also includes peoples whose countries have been snatched from them through annexation: Iraq annexing Kuwait and Libya annexing Chad are ready examples.

The second category, which is often the largest, are people who have been displaced from their home countries by war or civil strife. The third category recognizes people who cannot or will not return to their own countries because of the fear of persecution based on race, religion, national origin, or affiliation with certain social or political groups.

The United Nations classifies as *refugees* those who for one of the reasons outlined above live unprotected by the laws of a nation-state. A refugee is a person living outside his or her own country.

However, the United Nations and its member states don't accord refugee status to people fleeing from intolerable economic conditions unless they are the conditions of war. Even at this it's no guarantee. In 1979, Cambodia's rice harvest was destroyed as a result of war and Cambodians fled to Thailand but were not accorded refugee status. The Khmers were not protected by international convention that would insure them against involuntary repatriation, but by June 1979 Thailand, fearful of its own internal security, forced 42,000 Cambodians back to their home. This led to an international outcry forcing Thailand to open its borders to all Cambodians seeking refuge, but Thailand appealed to the United Nations for help.

The countries that are the sources of refugees have sometimes denied any domestic problem within their borders and have oftentimes branded the refugees as bandits, guerrilla fighters, or simply illegal but voluntary migrants. The governments of Cambodia, Afghanistan, and Vietnam have often dismissed the refugee status and claims by their citizens who seek refuge outside their borders.

International conventions acknowledge a moral obligation to admit bona fide refugees for asylum until repatriation or resettlement can be arranged. Countries on the receiving end have denied access to refugees as a device to avoid financial obligations. There are cases when the United States refused refugee migrants from Haiti but accepted 120,000 Cuban émigrés. Court cases were filed against the United States government, which eventually compromised by allowing both the Haitians and Cubans classifying them as *entrants,* thereby freeing itself from economic assistance to resettle them.

During the cold war when the Soviet Union was still communist, application for exit visas brought harassment from the government. Citizens who tried to emigrate for economic reasons were branded traitors and spies. This was also the case in East Germany during the time the Berlin Wall was standing. Exit visas were rarely given. One had to scale the fence. Those who succeeded were lucky; many never made it alive.

Some refugees flee with no intention to ever return to their homes, such as the boat people from Vietnam to the United States of America, people from the Soviet Union, and Asians who were expelled from Uganda during the Idi Amin regime. Sometimes people think they will return home, but, once they have settled down and find comfort, they stay. An influx of refugees may upset the ethnic balance within a state, which is why some countries refuse the entry of foreigners within their borders. Malaysia refused to give temporary asylum to Chinese citizens who fled from Vietnam.[53]

The United Nations has been unable to do much because independent states that are sovereign are safe from external interference from foreign countries. International law does not allow states to meddle in the domestic affairs of others, but now these laws are being looked at carefully again with a possibility of review.

This has been prompted by the acts of genocide going on in many countries around the globe, especially in Africa with the Sudanese government sponsoring genocide in Darfur. The government has armed

53 Kathleen Newland, A world of refugees, Topic issue No 132, p. 16.

the Arab men who ride horses and camels to kill the indigenous blacks. The horse riders are called the Janjaweed militiamen. They destroy and burn down the houses of the villagers, loot, and rape, making the Sudanese black tribesmen flee into neighboring towns. The displaced become refugees, and they are currently staying at various refugee camps.

During the Second World War, Germany's Hitler exterminated Jews in the genocidal manner, which horrified the world. However, at the end of the war the creation of the United Nations brought under its charter and convention the law on genocide. In 1948 it was signed by 127 countries. The signatories undertook to "prevent and punish" genocide, defined as deliberate extermination of a race of people.

The government in Sudan has been targeting three black African tribes that have defended themselves when possible by attacking the Arabs. The American Congress called the situation that of genocide, but the African Union disagrees.

This does not, however, matter much, for under international law there is no inherent right of armed humanitarian interventions, even to stop genocide. The United Nations charter only sanctions force in self–defense, which you find (under article 51 or when it is authorized to do so by the Security Council to avert a breach of the peace). The charter forbids intervention in matters that concern domestic internal issues, which are outside the jurisdiction of international law. But there are times the injunction can be overridden by a chapter VII authorization.

The Sudanese government threatened Britain and Australia "not to meddle" in its affairs when they offered to send peacekeeping troops. This proves that something sinister is going on, which they don't want any Western country to detect or uncover.

The head of Britain's armed forces offered to send in 5,000 British soldiers to stop the carnage where there are mass graves everywhere around the southern part of the country, the south of Sudan and Darfur where oil had been discovered. It is the Arab elite of the Nile that enjoy the rewards of a mineral found in the indigenous black region of Sudan, where the genocide is going on. The Sudanese government refused peacekeeping forces and threatened to mobilize the entire nation to fight back if the Western countries sent in their troops.

Things are so bad in Darfur that when survivor villagers were asked about the events, they said their neighbors were trussed with chains and burned alive. It did not take much effort for news reporters to get the facts: about a million people were terrorized into fleeing the embers of their huts. Like the aid workers, they know how the government blocks food supplies from getting to the displaced refugees, provoking the lukewarm African Union to voice its disapproval.

The question now most asked is this: Must intervention in such horrific situations be legal? The United Nations intervened in the past to stop gross violations of human rights in Somalia and Yugoslavia. But it could do so again. This would require a Security Council resolution, which China might veto because of Tibet, and Russia too might veto because of Chechnya, where domestic ethnic conflicts are still provoked from the two who want independence out of Russia and China.

Many governments, particularly poor and despotic ones, argue that national sovereignty should always supersede humanitarian issues. Most Western governments argue the opposite. In May 2006, despite the peace deal signed in Nigeria between the Sudanese government and Darfur rebels, the conflict persisted. The African Union had no impact and influence to end the misery.

After the death of an estimated 300,000 and displacement of about two million people, Darfur rebels refused to sign the pact in Nigeria and went back to fighting.

Another summit of African leaders under the African Union took place in Gambia, with the hope that the Sudanese government would agree to 15,000 peacekeepers under the UN's commission, backed by NATO air support and strategic intelligence to replace the African Union's 7,000 troops. This was bluntly refused by the Sudanese government.

In 1994, a collective insanity crept into the African country of Rwanda when the Hutu ethnic group descended on its Tutsi fellow brothers and Hutu sympathizers who tried to protest the gruesome murder of Tutsis. It is still unbelievable today that within three months 800,000 people were killed.

The university where you expect to have the most civilized people turned out to be worse: a horror chamber where more than five hundred staff and students were murdered within a two-week period with a few escaping to tell the tale in Congo and Burundi. Many of the students were killed by their lecturers.

The number that participated was too high for all to be punished so the ring leaders were singled out and tried by an International Court of Justice.

President Paul Kagame's government brought an end to the genocide through the help of his own rebel group, the Rwandan Patriotic Front that forced an end to the genocide in 1994. They agreed to drop the ethnic group recognition. There would be no more Hutus and Tutsis—only Rwandans as Hutus and Tutsis had eventually participated in the genocide. Rwanda is the only genocide case where the victims, the Tutsis, chose to reintegrate their killers into the country and to live as neighbors again.[54]

Fifteen years after the horrific wars in Rwanda, where 800,000 Tutsis and moderate Hutus were exterminated by genocide, there is no international institution with the capacity to respond quickly to mass killing of civilians.

The International Criminal Court was created by the Rome statute in 1998 and began work in 2003 with the aim of preventing crimes against humanity, genocide, and war crimes.

Luis Moreno-Ocampo is the chief prosecutor of the International Criminal Court, a veteran Argentine lawyer in his mid-sixties. He is a stateless prosecutor and knows it to be a difficult challenge. He has about one hundred states under his jurisdiction but not a single policeman. The prospect of prosecuting war criminals in Darfur and elsewhere will deter others from committing horrific crimes. Genocides "are planned crimes," Ocampo declared.

In the 1990s, the wars that resulted in horrific massacres in Rwanda, Bosnia, Chechnya, Liberia, Congo, and Sierra Leone swept the world on the path of bloodshed and genocide. While the killings went on, the international body pushed for laws that would make the perpetrators accountable before the law. The Rome statute was endorsed by 120 countries and the revolution started in the history of nations. World leaders agreed to be held accountable for war crimes against humanity and genocide. Investigators would work with prosecutors to get the criminals prosecuted. Prisons would hold those convicted.

Few states voted against the treaty: Iraq Israel, Libya, China, and the United States. But a few hours before the deadline, President Bill Clinton signed the treaty, a necessary step before Senate ratification.

---

54 The Economist, April 11th, 2009, "The Genocide in Rwanda." p. 36,

A few weeks later, President George Bush, his successor, declared his government would not recognize the signature and declared international treaties as tools for the weak. After the 9/11 attacks and precisely in May 2002, John R. Bolton, who was under secretary of State, sent a letter to Kofi Annan, who was secretary-general of the United Nations, announcing that the United States did not consider itself bound by the Rome statute. President Bush went further to sign into law the American Service-Members Protection Act, which requires American forces to liberate any American in ICC custody, popularly called The Hague Invasion Act.

The Hague has been home to the International Court of Justice or World Court, a legal arm of the United Nations. During the Yugoslav wars, a tribunal was set up and has since looked into 161 cases against individuals, including Slobodan Milosevic, the former head of state, for genocide. The Hague has become a symbol of both the promise of international law and its shortcomings.[55]

The International Criminal Court had issued the warrant of arrest for Sudan's Omar al Bashir for war crimes in Darfur on the fourth of March, 2009, for acts of genocide, but today he is yet to be arrested. The African Union is a bit divided on the issue since many leaders still belong to the class to despots that might engage in such crimes. There was, however, a referendum in 2011 and it was successful, and was monitored by the United Nations with over 90 percent of the votes in favor of forming a new state. This has made the south of Sudan independent from the North of Sudan.[56] When conflicts of this nature take place in a country and diplomacy has failed to stop the carnage, the international community often applies sanctions on the country urging countries and nations across the globe not to engage in business transactions with the defaulter. Sanctions isolate, ignore, and chastise, but many times they have not been very effective on countries that produce oil. This is because many nations have joined the oil-thirsty group including China, and they are all dependent on oil to run their economies and society.

When the G8 countries agreed to bring sanctions on Sudan and

55 Elizabeth Rubin, "If not peace, then justice", The New York Times Magazine, April 2nd, 2006, p. 43.

56 Patrick Smith, "Crime without punishment", "Rwanda/Sudan: The Africa Report No 16, April–May, 2009, p. 54

Zimbabwe, for example, the Chinese government was very reluctant and continued to do business with the countries concerned.

China today is now the third largest economy in the world after the United States of America and Japan. China has ignored the human rights abuses on the African continent and has continued to trade with the sanctioned countries, selling them arms and all necessary commodities they need. The Chinese government declared the principles of peaceful coexistence to include mutual territorial respect, nonaggression, and noninterference in each other's internal affairs. This has satisfied most African governments.

African leaders feel Western examples of democracy, which include presidential tenure and types of public institutions, are often not suitable for some African conditions. Many African countries are faced with internal conflicts, others are not economically viable states and are facing poverty, and some others have to balance class and ethnic divisions. This makes every society and culture unique, requiring their own internal solutions to governing their states effectively. China is believed to have gone through its own difficulties, which it has worked out. These include a strong, focused central government, limited democracy, powerful state-owned enterprises, and long-term development plans. China's noninterference policy suits African leaders who are eager to do business with the new leader in the continent.[57]

Despite the sanctions from America, Sudan is among the fastest-growing economies in Africa. Inflation has been kept low and it has had a GDP of 8 percent growth since 2005, which they have maintained. They have managed their economy well, but it is mostly the Arab region that prospers. The central government in Khartoum is where they built the paradise city like in Dubai. The other regions are poor neglected, and many don't have electricity.[58]

The question that still bothers all right-thinking people is the position of noninterference in domestic matters of a country even when a genocide is taking place with hundreds of thousands murdered in cold blood.

George W. Bush declared that the Geneva Conventions needed a review with the recent happening where he felt the protections given

57 Anver Versi, A meeting of minds and needs, African Business, July 2006, p. 17

58 The Economist, August 5, 2006, p. 36.

to prisoners could not be extended to terrorists and suicide bombers. He concluded that al-Qaeda members do not qualify as lawful enemy combatants. He said at the time, "We are fighting a new kind of war and a new kind of enemy. I believe time will tell that he was right."

"Under the Geneva Conventions, a combatant is deemed lawful and therefore entitled to prisoner-of-war status and protection if he is a member of either a regular government force or an organized militia wearing a distinctive sign, carrying arms openly and abiding by the rules of war. As such, he may refuse to give his captors any information save his name rank and serial number and if charged would be entitled to a trial by a normal court martial." This is provided in article 3 of the Geneva Conventions.[59]

The government administration of President George W. Bush polarized emotions when he unilaterally went into Iraq without the United Nations' approval. He was expected to have used the multilateral approach, which meant getting the consent of all G8 members and also the Security Council. Multilateralism is not a slogan; it means when a violator breaks the rule, he must pay. Whether it be criminal justice or nuclear nonproliferation, impunity is not seen as an option. The European Union had placed effective multilateralism at the center of European security strategy in December 2003.

Most of the European Union countries declared that if America would get support to fight the terrorist group, they had to involve all by using multilateralism as the option, which means America must trust the European Union where they confronted similar enemies. In the cases of radical nations like Iran, the European Union felt sanctions and a political option of offering alternatives to getting a peaceful settlement of conflicts would be better. The need to join efforts together to reform the international institutions, like the United Nations and its various agencies like NATO after the Second World War ended almost seven decades ago is necessary.

Former President, Jimmy Carter, the ethicist, had argued for a principled polity. He believes that America as the only superpower left must set an example where the world would feel reassured of its commitment to moral values.

He feels America should be neutral and work as the peacemaker for nations in conflict. This, he believes, would make warring factions

59 The Economist, June 9, 2007, p. 51.

look up to the United States and head to Washington for help. This might work in certain cases, but when it comes to a case like genocide, what would Washington then do if, after negotiations and persuasion through diplomatic channels, negotiations failed? What would be the next step? Sanctions have not helped. The only option would be to go in and stop the mess as George Bush did, which sent warning signals to other despotic leaders in Africa; Libya has now changed its aggressive stance toward the United States and the entire West; its governing style was also toned down. This had been achievable because of the regime change in Iraq and Afghanistan.

It is a known fact that despotic leaders are stubborn and difficult to deal with through the diplomatic channel. This approach has failed in the many African countries engaged in devastating wars that go on for years. "America has to be the sledge hammer at times that squashes stubborn bugs." This is by intervention of the military. The dictators and despots around the world who have been involved in genocide and mass murders have taken advantage of all the weaknesses of international law, which forbids on many occasions domestic interference within the borders of a sovereign country.

The acts of genocide and the blood of the innocent cry out for review of international law to cope with the supersonic age of the millennium decade, where the disadvantaged groups all over the world want a stake in the governance of their states. But because of the systems of government being practiced, they have been kept out of the ruler ship class. To get power, they have formed religious groups and want to overthrow the established systems, accusing them of Western ideals. What the al-Qaeda, Taliban, and Boko Haram want is to get into government and take over, forming a theocratic government where they become the new ruling class in the name of religion. In Nigeria, the late President Umaru Yar'Adua had realized this and asked the security operatives to crush them to death. Many others did not understand and started asking that they be spared. But because he was a northerner and Muslim, the people of the northern region of Nigeria kept mute while the press and southerners asked that they be spared. It was a fundamental mistake as they continued the havoc of killing the innocent; even their Muslim brothers who are seen as moderates have not been spared.[60]

60 The Punch, Vol 17, No 20 450 August 4 2009, p. 2

The United States of America did more than any other nation to make the world a better place when Europe dominated the world with Her Majesty's government as the most powerful in the world. Asia and Africa were subjugated, but, after the Second World War, America took charge, liberating Asia and Africa by convincing Winston Churchill to extend freedom to the colonies of Africa, which eventually led to the independence of the states in Africa.

The United States remains the world's defining power; its decisions guide the rules and nations follow. It must today redefine the global polity by addressing the threats that divide the global village, from religious extremism to nuclear proliferation and armament. The United States must also play the leadership role for climate stability and international finance. Independent states that are sovereign need to abide by certain responsibilities.

At the United Nations summit conference in 2005, the international community declared that it had a "responsibility to protect" citizens of all countries around the world from genocide.

This marked an important stage in the debate about human rights and national power. States were expected to protect their citizens and populations, and if they failed to do so, the international community would step in. This has still failed to achieve international consensus on when and how to intervene.

This is also a result in the failure to agree among the states that work through multilateral action. Darfur today has two million displaced citizens who are refugees, and four million are on food aid.

The world leaders must forge and agree on a stronger international consensus to combat the spread of nuclear materials as no one has the right to set off a nuclear arms race. Despite the global economic boom, poverty is high in developing economies and the inequality gap increases. This fuels resentment on which extremism thrives. World leaders across the globe, including Nigeria, must strive to meet the millennium development goals. The global bodies, including the United Nations and World Bank that were created after the Second World War ended in 1945, must today upgrade their rules and laws to

---

The Nation August 5th, 2009 vol 3 No 1111
The Nation August 1st (Saturday) 2009
Daily Sun March 30th 2010. P. 13.
The Guardian Thursday July 30, 2009

adapt to the changing power equation and the new threats to security, prosperity, and peace, including the effects of climate change and the dangers of global terrorism.

The former United States President Ronald Reagan addressed the British Parliament twenty-five years ago. He said cynics may roll their eyes when a US president calls for a "crusade for freedom that will engage the faith and fortitude of the next generation or implores allies to move toward a world in which all people are free to determine their own destiny." But America's greatness and standing in the world will ultimately be determined by the extent to which it champions those words and tries to advance them.

Today as we face conflicts everywhere, including those of terrorism, Ronald Reagan had also said that weakness encourages aggression and that the best way to achieve peace is through strength.

The United States of America is a peaceful nation that wants peace. It does not go to war because it wants to, but because the terrorists provoked it and declared war. The United States had to respond.

The Islamic extremists have been fighting the international community since the early 1970s. It has taken the world years and a devastating attack on US soil for all to recognize the truth.[61] The bitter hatred started when the Palestinians were displaced from their land. In 1914, more than 600,000 Arabs lived in Palestine. After the extermination of Jews by Adolf Hitler's Nazi regime during the Second World War, the nation of Israel was created in 1948 from the ashes of the Holocaust. And from then on, there has been no peace. The surrounding states are Arab states that detest the Israelis. The capture of East Jerusalem, the West Bank, and Gaza in the Six-Day War in 1967 made Palestinian Arabs and their Middle East counterparts dislike the Israeli Jews, and these Arabs have felt America's support for the Israeli people. This has brought about an anti-American stance from Hamas and Muslim radicals like Hezbollah who feel America is pro-Israel.

The world must continue to work together through the established agencies of the United Nations to see how radicals and despotic regimes can be managed during periods when conflicts arise. This is to prevent the heavy carnage that comes with such conflicts.

The countries of the Middle East have to change the confrontational attitude and prove to the world that their societies are advanced

61 Rudolph Gulianna, Newsweek, Special edition, 2008, p. 39

psychologically and would govern their societies peacefully and more democratically before the world can be convinced they can handle nuclear weapons. This, however, is currently not the position. Violence does no good to any nation.

Iran has just recently exported through two of its citizen's weapons of mass destruction and death into Nigeria with the vigilant security operatives intercepting it. This was reported to the Security Council in the United Nations.

The Republicans feel in America that Democrats in Congress can't be allowed to play politics with the national security of the United States. Tehran's quest for weapons of mass destruction, its support for terrorism, its antagonism toward Israel and the peace process, and its repression of domestic freedom and rights have been the style of the clerical regime's policy since its inception in 1979. The terrorists are fighting around different parts of the world where you have Muslims who want to overthrow the various governments and introduce their own clerics and theocratic governments. If the democratic governments are not vigilant, their regimes will be overthrown in religious coups that establish Islamic theocracies.

Chapter Six

Germany and World War I

The unification of Germany in 1871 led to its interest on the issue of African colonies. Germany had been a late entrant in the quest for African colonies. Chancellor Otto Von Bismarck was more interested in the unification of Germany and the strategic role it could play in European politics.

Lobby groups included West German Society for Colonization and Export, which was established in 1881 and the Central Association for Commercial Geography and the Promotion of German Interests Abroad, which was established in 1878. They convinced the government to join the race for colonies to improve the economic interests of the German state.

Bismarck discovered owning colonies helped to stabilize the domestic politics and enhanced the economy. This led to the Berlin conference of 1884–1885, hosted by Germany. The conference led to a watershed in Africa.[62] It proclaimed that for effective claim to a territory, physical occupation was necessary. This led to the scramble and partition for African territories. Germany colonized South-West Africa (present-day Namibia), German East Africa (present-day Rwanda, Burundi, and Tanzania), Togo, and the Cameroons very near the Bakkasi territory of Nigeria.

62 http://encyclopedia.Jrank.org/artcles/pages/5926/Africa-German – Colonies html.

The Germans had established formal institutions and structures to support the colonial government in the new territories. The policy administered was that of ruthlessness, racial supremacy, and economic dispossession of the indigenous population. German South-West Africa best exemplifies a colonial situation in which race constituted a group identity with certain predetermined advantages.

The structure of governance in the colonies had the governor as head who controlled the colony but was getting his directive from Berlin. There were civilian officials and the commanders of the armed forces in the colony. The armed forces were answerable to the governor who got his orders from Berlin. The military acted as defense for security, and there were also regional administrators. They ruled by direct and indirect rules as the need arose. It was a difficult task running the colonies as many competing interests brought conflict that the governor had to mediate.

The African chiefs were next to the colonial officials in rank and importance. They were subject to German authority. Their loyalty was to the appointing colonial authority. They served at the pleasure of the colonial authority and were responsible for tax collection and getting labor for colonial projects. Race was a critical determinant, and all Africans were below in rank to any European.

German interests were promoted while African political, economic, and socio-cultural interests were sacrificed through racial prejudice. German colonists were projected as members of the superior and enlightened race, while the natives like the Herero and Nama communities were depicted as inferior, indolent, and destined to be permanent subjects and servants.

The German policy was detested, leading to revolts from the Herero in 1904. The Germans overreacted like they did later with the Jews, exterminating 60,000 people out of a population of 80,000. The Germans did not only shoot their victims, but they also poisoned their wells, resulting in the high death rate.

The Nama experienced similar fates during the Maji Maji Uprising (1905–1907) in other German colonies in southeast Africa, where the Germans destroyed the crops and livestock through a scorched-earth policy leading to of the deaths of approximately 75,000 people. Germans had crushed all forms of uprising in the colonies.

The Germans used brute force on their subjects, believing might is right. They said their interests reigned supreme and had used the color of their skin to claim superiority, thereby subjugating the African.[63]

However, because not many women came down to Africa from Europe, the white men had no choice but to cohabit with African women, posing a major threat to white superiority. The miscegenation undermined the perceived order of white superiority by the creation of mulattoes who defied classification—they were neither white nor black. The intermarriage lowered the status of those who got involved in the union and were accused of undermining their own race.

The case of racial purity was defended on the grounds of preserving white status. In order to maintain the class status, the marriages were stigmatized and those involved were regarded as deviants.

The German officials sought to ensure conformity to the norms of segregated society maintenance of the status quo, which was anchored in racially divided societies, political hegemony, economic superiority, and elitism.

Africans at the time were seen to be inferior, based on racism, and as a result race determined the verdict of court judgments in Africa at the time. You could not take a white man to court then and expect to win, even if you were not the guilty party.

The colonial office acted as mediator in times of conflict in the colonies. The Germans saw Africans at the time as semi-apes and felt nothing good could come out of the Africans. They used brute force and coerced labor in running the German colonies, which resulted in intense criticism of Germany's colonial policy.[64]

The Germans built a few railroads with the aims of boosting the economies of the colonies for the benefit of the home country. They developed hospitals and educational institutions. The German colonies were not, however, as advanced as the British colonies who developed better governing systems to encourage the Africans to be able to run their own affairs in preparation for self-government.

However, by 1914 an ill wind blew over the European continent, which had been caused by different rivalries and jealousies among the

63 Ibid

64 Ibid

various countries in Europe. The British and Germans were competing among themselves for the most powerful navy in the world, bringing tension to the European continent.

Many European countries, having discovered the economic gains from African territories, started competing for colonies in Africa, causing minor conflicts. This exposed the unfriendly disposition the European countries had among themselves. The French did not trust the Germans because of a war Germany had won years back in 1871.

Then there was the new patriotism within nations where citizens felt the drive to be loyal to their nations, which brought nationalism. Some other countries were power drunk and felt they could take on other nations. There were also the annexed nations that wanted their independence. The drive by powerful nations for expansionist adventures brought about conflicts as weaker nations got annexed, such was with the breakup of the Ottoman Empire in Eastern Europe and the loss of Alsace-Lorraine by France to Germany during the 1870s.

This led to the Slavic independence movements in areas such as Bulgaria, and Serbia. The Serbian and Austrian relationship was very tense at the time when Austria asked for an independent Albania, thus preventing Serbia from its expansionist move into the Adriatic regions during the early 1900s. The aggressive movement brought tension between Russia and Austria, and when Russia supported the independence movement of the Slavs, Turkey then backed Austria to gain Austrian support.

In Western Europe, the loss of Alsace-Lorraine by France to Germany in 1871 brought the feeling of animosity between the two nations. The kaiser's self-proclaimed slogan that Germany "had a place in the sun" worsened the tensions as an arms buildup began. German naval power became a threat to the British government, which led to the alliance between Britain and France.

The disputes over various territories continued to bring tensions between various countries, especially the African territory of Morocco, including the Anglo-French-German Agadir Crisis of July 1911, and the Austrian annexation of Bosnia-Herzegovina, which was a region populated by Bosniaks (Muslims) in 1908. This was called the Balkan Crisis.

Germany's military strength was increased and it introduced the gunboat diplomacy of meddling and conflicting alliances. Imperialism, nationalism, and expansionist drives in the last days of colonialism triggered of tensions that led to the First World War. The arms race began among all nations who started building their military strengths, which included the navy and air force. No country wanted to lag behind. These long-term feuds and conflicts brought about the Triple Entente in which England, France, and Russia created a common alliance opposed to the Triple Alliance of Germany, Austria-Hungary, and Italy.

Then the final blow that triggered the war was the assassination of Archduke Franz Ferdinand and his wife. He was heir to the Austrian throne. Serbian Black Hand terrorists in Sarajevo did the dastardly act on June 28, 1914. This sparked a big crisis that was not handled properly by all parties involved in the peaceful settlement. Britain proposed a peace treaty, which was rejected by Austria and Germany on the twenty-sixth of July, 1914. Instead of trying to settle things between Austria and Serbia, Germany wanted a cause for war by escalating and prompting the Austrians with a blank check whereby Austria gave an ultimatum to Serbia that was turned down by Serbia. The Austrians had been in conflict with Serbia from some past disputes. Germany prompted Austria further to give unconditional support on its actions against Serbia, which finally triggered the First World War.[65]

Austria and the Ottoman Empire declared war on Serbia. This caused Russia and France to declare war on both of them. And this led to Germany declaring war on Russia and France, which had an alliance with Britain. The Germans needed to go through Belgium to get into France so they invaded Belgium, breaching the neutrality guarantee of the country, which outraged the British who now declared war on the Central Powers.

During World War I, British, French, and Belgian forces in Africa successfully defeated territories held by Germany in Africa. However, in Germany's east Africa territories the case was different. General Paul von Lettow-Vorbeck, with 4,000 German and 12,000 African Askari forces, kept 250,000 British troops at bay. The allies had said earlier that they were not interested in annexing colonial territories, which they still kept to. But by the fifth of November, 1918, in a pre-Armistice

65 http://wiki.answers.com/Q/what caused World War I. p. 1-3

declaration when Germany decided to surrender, the Allies eventually took the German African colonial territories.

The peace negotiations exposed the intentions of the Allies to retain German African colonial territories. The Paris Peace Conference, which was written into the covenant of the League of Nations, was signed on June 28, 1919. The covenant highlighted the collective security of member states, international arbitration limitations on arms, and the distribution of German colonies in Africa through a mandate system whereby the territories would be shared among the allied powers and held in trust.

The most important treaty signed at Versailles was that of 1919. It was the most important among the five peace treaties that terminated the First World War. The other four were Saint Germain for Austria, Trianon for Hungary, Neuilly for Bulgaria, and Sevres for Turkey. The outstanding figures in the negotiations were called "the big four." Woodrow Wilson represented the United States of America, George Clemenceau for France, David Lloyd George represented England, and Emanuele Orlando for Italy. Germany was defeated and needed no consultation.

Woodrow Wilson's main objective was the creation of states based on the principles of self–determination, and the formation of the League of Nations was embodied in the treaty. The treaty had blamed Germany for the outbreak of the war and imposed the payment of reparations.

The main territorial clauses were those recommending the return of Alsace and Lorraine to France, placing former German colonies in Africa under the League of Nations as mandates, giving West Prussia, including Poznan and the Polish Corridor, back to Poland, establishing Danzig as a free city, and setting up plebiscites that resulted in the transfer of Eupen and Malmedy to Belgium, Schleswig to Denmark, and parts of Upper Silesia to Poland. The Saar Territory came under French rule for fifteen years. The Rhineland was to be occupied by the allies for fifteen years, and the right bank of the Rhine was to be permanently demilitarized. The German military was reduced to a maximum of 100,000 soldiers, including the German Navy. Germany was forbidden to build major weapons of aggression. After futile protests, Germany accepted its fate, which became effective from January 1920.

The League of Nations had in its covenants the workings of how the mandated territories would be classified. This was written in article

22 of the covenant where there was class A, B, and C mandates. Article 23 further described the human rights those living in and who governed the territory would follow. The mandating powers were required to bring justice and fairness to the inhabitants of the territories they controlled, bring fair and humane conditions of labor for men, women, and children, and maintain public order and morals. And they were required to guarantee freedom of conscience and religion, bring an end to slavery, limit military development, and take steps to prevent disease.

The Class Mandates

The class A mandates territory was considered advanced enough politically and economically that a provisional independence could be granted. The African colonies did not qualify as they were not advanced yet. But the former Turkish provinces of Iraq, Syria, Lebanon, and Palestine were in this category. The class A mandates got their independence as early as 1949.

The League of Nations' class B mandates was placed under the administration of the League of Nations. The African colonial territories fell under this categorization. They were not advanced enough politically or economically for independence.

The mandates were given guidelines that there should be no military training of the natives or military buildup except for policing and defense. This form of mandate applied especially to the former German colonies and protectorates in Africa: Togoland, Kamerun (Cameroon), and German East Africa. Togoland was shared between France and Britain. It was split one-third to two-thirds along the north-south line on July 20, 1922. The one-third to the west became British Togoland and was administered from the Gold Coast. The two-thirds to the east became French Togo and became part of French West Africa.

Cameroon, called Kamerun at the time, was mandated to France with two small sections on the northwest border with Nigeria being administered by Britain. The British Cameroon was neglected. There was then Germany's east Africa colonies of Tanganyika, administered to Britain, and the small territory of Ruanda-Urundi (now called Rwanda and Burundi) mandated to Belgium on August 31, 1923. In 1925, Belgium formed an administrative union between the mandate it had for Ruanda-Urundi and the Belgian Congo. A small triangle of land to the south of German East Africa, the Kionga Triangle, was given to Portugal, which was added to its colony of Mozambique.

League of Nations class C mandates were states not capable of sustaining independence due to sparse populations, small size, or remoteness. German South-West Africa, today's Namibia, was given on October 1, 1922, as a class C mandate to the Union of South Africa. New Guinea was mandated to Australia, Western Samoa to New Zealand, and the northwestern Pacific islands of Caroline, Marshall, Marianne, and Pelew Islands to Japan. The mandates were in theory run by the League of Nations but in reality were controlled by the country mandated to hold trust.

After the First World War with the devastating effects, the world was thrown into an economic crisis a decade later when in 1929 the Great Depression took place. This affected many of the world powers, but those that had colonies in Africa had an edge where they could get some of their raw materials at subsidized rates. This led to the clamor in Germany for the return of its African colonies. But other nations without colonies turned to wise financial prudence, and all survived the period.

Chapter Seven

Why German Colonies in Africa Were Seized and World War II

In January 1933, a new dawn began when the destiny of Germany fell into the hands of Adolf Hitler, an autocratic leader. Hitler believed in the superiority of Nordic and Aryan race, a theory debunked by scientists and rejected by philosophers. It was an anathema to theologians, which the world at large saw as repugnant. He believed the African was just a semi-ape.

Hitler was a member of the National Socialist Party, which controlled Germany between 1933 and 1945. He believed facts of any event should be twisted at any moment by people who were worthy to be leaders in a country. He used propaganda in a skillful way to persuade people. He believed people should lie on a grand scale. He believed there was a certain element of credibility in the magnitude of a lie. He was of the opinion that the masses of people in a nation were more corrupt than we thought consciously. Hitler believed that in the simplicity of their souls they fell victim to a big lie more so than to small ones. Since human beings tell small lies, they will be too ashamed to tell unduly big lies.[66]

The human soul meant nothing to Hitler. He was bloody minded to a horrifying degree. His book *Mein Kampf* was full of violence,

---

66 F. S Joelson, Germany's claim to colonies, Hurst & Blackett, Ltd. June 1939.

attacks, brutality, terror, intolerance, hate, fanaticism, extermination, and ferocious utterances.

At the beginning of his reign in Germany, he declared that Germany was not interested in the African colonies anymore, but he kept on contradicting himself in later years. He declared Germany's future was not in Africa, and that his territorial policy could not find its fulfillment in the Cameroons but in Europe. He said the colonies were not suitable for European settlement.

He maltreated the Jews who had served in various capacities in Germany, either in time of war or in time of peace. All Jews got the same treatment, even those who had risen to positions of eminence. He rounded them up and exterminated them through genocide. He ordered the persecution, which started with notices placed and hanging outside hotels, shops, and swimming pools that said, "Jews not desired." The inscriptions were put everywhere. This act of barbarism of Hitler and his agents was what stirred the national conscience of people where all shades of political opinion decided it unwise to hand over the African territory and former German colonies to Nazism. They felt they could not afford to return the German colonies to Germany.

It was the extermination of the Jews that brought international recognition to the danger of having the swastika in Africa. Nazism had to be barred. It was discriminatory, racial, terroristic, and militaristic with a doctrine of racial superiority. It approved the use of brute force and, in Hitler's words, "In eternal peace humanity perishes."[67]

Africa had been described as savage because of the barbarity the Europeans discovered in the various customs and beliefs across the continent and also the intertribal wars that often took place, leading to destruction of populations.

Germany under the Nazi regime of Hitler tried to reestablish in the Reich tribalism, which Africa was modifying and abandoning at the time.

The major world powers who had taken over the German territories and colonies after the end of the First World War had refused a surrender of the colonies to Germany. They had various reasons as they saw Germany on a warpath. They saw the danger of Hitlerism in Africa and felt the Africans would be ideal material for enslavement as they were easygoing and had not developed where they could be

67 Ibid

independent minded and as they had no experience of government at the time. It was not ideal for Germany to get back the territories. Hitler was a hard task master and slave driver and a great threat to world peace. Germany had proved unsuitable for the development of African territories because minorities had been crushed within its own frontiers, and also because of the war-minded nature of Hitler who breached all international obligations and treaties and allowed the denial of human rights within its borders.

This style of governance contradicted the principles embodied in the mandates, which constituted the most powerful and rational argument against confiding African colonies back to Germany. It was believed African inhabitants would be disadvantaged with Germany as their colonial master, as against the British or French or any other power within the League of Nations.

The Germans were denied the control of their former African colonies. The reason was that it would use them as submarine bases, arm the blacks, and use the colonies as bases of intrigue. Germany would treat the natives badly.

Germany, on the other hand, continued to assert that because of the downturn in the economy it needed access to tropical raw materials and also space for the expansion of its population. The country further asserted that, under the principles of peace, the conquest of the league did not give them equitable title to its colonies. The allied countries that formed the league rejected every defense of the Germans in holding on to German colonies in Africa. The allies brought in the vote of United States, asserting they felt compelled to safeguard their security and the peace of the world, which was threatened by the military imperialism of a Germany that had sought to establish bases where it could pursue a policy of intimidation and interference aimed at other countries.

The Allied powers considered the loss to amount only to about 3 percent of German economic output as the colonies were not producing much. The Treaty of Versailles in article 119 states that "Germany renounces in favor of the principal Allied and Associated Powers all its rights and titles, over its overseas possession." No clause of any treaty could be more explicit.

It provides for outright and final renunciation of all rights, not a qualified and temporary transfer of some right. The surrender was as explicit as that of Alsace and Lorraine to France; southern Tyrol, the

Trentino, and Trieste to Italy; and Eupen and Malmedy to Belgium. Lord Balfour, one of the original signatories of the covenant, said the following when addressing the league on May 17, 1922.

Mandates are not creation of the league and they cannot in substance be altered by the league. The league's duties are confined to seeing that the specific and detailed terms of the mandates are in accordance with the decisions taken by the Allied and Associated Powers. Mr. Armey who was secretary of state for the colonies wrote in 1934 in eastern Africa Today and Tomorrow. The mandate is not a tenure from the League of Nations. It is only an undertaking on our part towards the league as to the lines on which we have decided to govern one of the territories surrendered, for good and all by Germany, and divided equally for good and all, by the Allied and Associated Powers. Beyond that undertaking we have no obligations towards the league and are free to do anything we like.

The permanent mandates commissions decided that a mandate was terminable when a country achieved a state of civilization, qualifying it to be independent and fulfilling a long list of stipulated conditions, and that the council of the league was the body competent to effect termination that the request should come in the first instance from the mandatory power.

Franz Kolbe, a publicist in the front rank, wrote the following in *Deutsche Politik.*

> "If German Mittel Afrika takes shape and our former colonies are restored to us, German central Africa, adequately supplied with munitions, could hold out for the longest war. The larger this German colonial empire in Mittel Afrika, the greater part it will play in future naval warfare on the supposition that the most important harbors, Duala (which is very close to the Bakassi region of Nigeria) Dares salaam, etc. are equipped as naval bases. The fortification of half the west Coast of West Africa could be a dangerous zone. Possibility of naval bases by means of fortification of half the west Coast would spell disaster for the opposition. As soon as the Suez Canal in another war is blocked against England the whole traffic between England and India, Australia and South Africa must go round the Cape which means that the

> whole of the maritime traffic would have to pass the Coast of German Mittel Afrika. What would be the result? It would be impossible for England to continue to concentrate its whole fleet in the North Sea and threaten Germany. She would be compelled to station a fairly large fleet in South Africa to safeguard its commerce and so considerably weaken its naval fighting forces in European waters."[68]

Thus the great lines of communication between England and these colonies will become vital arteries for the British Empire, which we can threaten most seriously from East and West Africa.

Mittel Afrika would lie more or less in the center of the British Empire and Australia and India would have to reckon with this German colony in their big trade enterprises. The policy of Mittel Afrika would have strong influences on that of Australia and India and therefore on that of Japan too. Through Mittel Afrika, we should really take our place as a world power with a great effect on South America, the Indian Ocean, and the Arab nations of North Africa. Mittel Afrika gives us a far more secure position as against the Anglo Saxon than does the Flanders coast, which has no value without Boulogne.

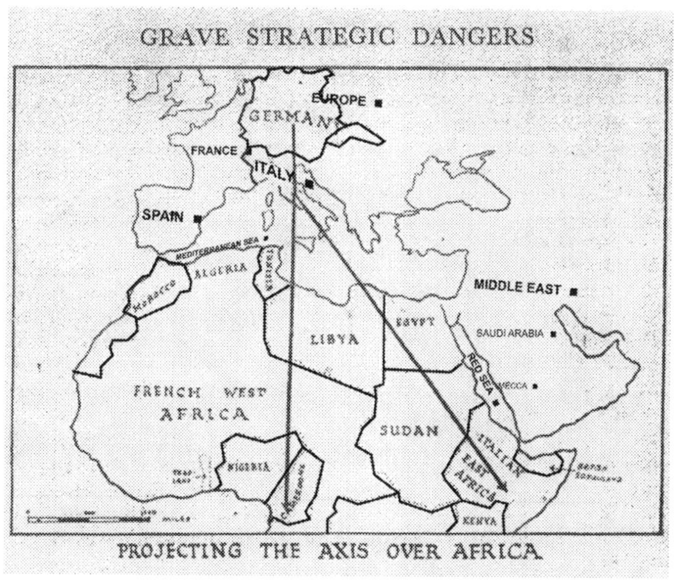

68 Ibid

A great German Mittel Afrika on a war footing will not only be able to maintain itself against attack from South Africa, India, and Australia, but in conjunction with the Arabs of North Africa will represent a power with which England will be in no hurry to pick a quarrel.

Two decades after the First World War, by 1938, the world had made its decision not to entrust to a defeated Germany anything that had to do with transoceanic territories from Africa, which could disrupt the peaceful region and upset the balance and safety of sea routes. The Allied powers maintained the status quo; the German territories had to remain confiscated, if the world would remain peaceful.

That was the decision and agreement after the First World War when the Germans surrendered. It was then unthinkable that Germany would renounce the decision in favor of the protesting Nazi regime that was even more antagonistic and militaristic than the Junker Germany of Hohenzollerns.

Hitler's regime was acquisitive and organized in a boastful way toward a warpath. The regime rearmed itself with aerial weapons, which if launched from the former African colonies would bring havoc to the great centers in the south, east, and western parts of Africa, destroying towns, railway, bridges, ports, mines, and shipping at sea.

It was believed at the time that the Allied powers would be incapacitated no matter how powerful they were because the Germans would use the opportunity to strike at night and destroy their targets by dawn.

The Allied powers who now held the colonies of Germany under the mandate had come to the conclusion that it would be a strategic error against France, and the free nations of the world, to allow the swastika to be hoisted in Africa, either in the east or west, especially when the world was being threatened by the shadow of a war Germany might trigger. Germany under Hitler was willing to use force and might over right, and in view of the air and naval power of Italy and its annexation of Ethiopia, and the Japanese expansion, the possibility was that these three members of the Anti-Comintern Pact, who were against Britain, may become aligned against the democracies.

The debate continued in admitting the Germans back in their African colonies under "guarantees" that it would abstain from the creation of black armies and naval and air bases, but the failures of safeguards to ensure the enforcement continued to stall the implementation of the handover. Nobody could guarantee that the *Germans* would not convert the colonies in Africa to bases and restrict their activities to that of peace.

The Germans were just not trusted at this period even if they were to pledge their word. Who could dare count on its obedience and adherence to it? All the states that were within striking distances of German zones would need an increased budget for their defence and should still expect to be in mortal danger from the threat of Germany.

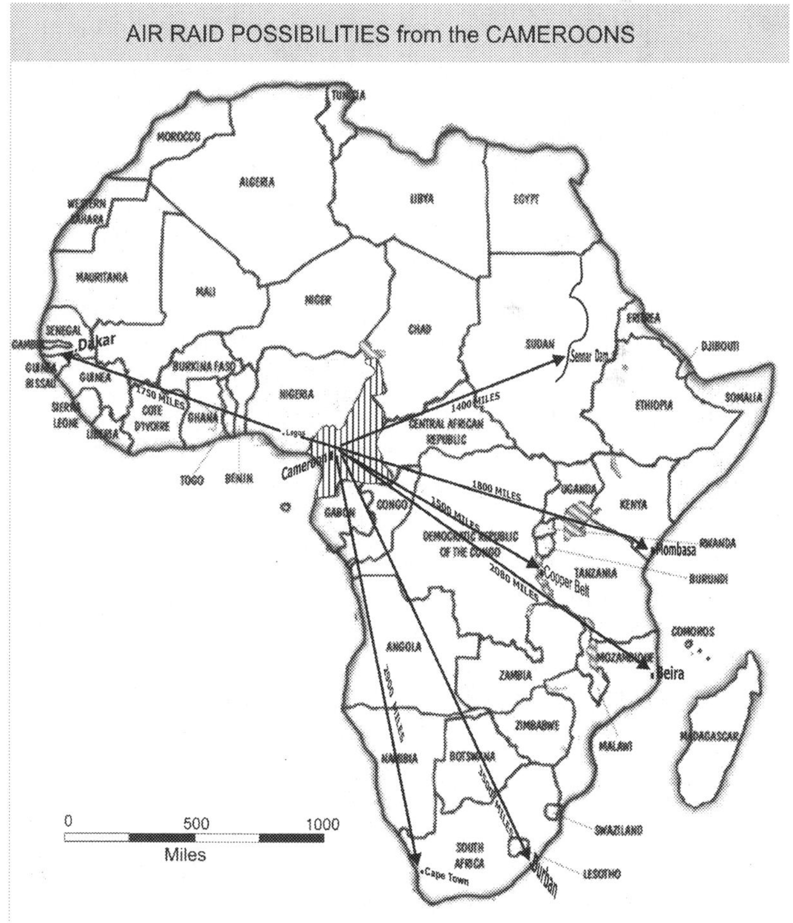

These included all the British territories, colonies, protectorates, and mandated regions in east, central, and West Africa. The self-governing colony of Southern Rhodesia, the Dominions of South Africa. And the French, Belgian, and Portuguese possessions had no fantasy of buying peace. They knew that such an agreement was the prelude to war. The foreign policy of Britain has been the protection of its vital communication by sea, and this was at a great risk if the Germans got back their African colonies.

The Germans had seen the African colonies as a stepping stone to world hegemony. The retrocession of Cameroon to Germany would provide excellent harborage that exists in the Cameroon River leading to Duala, which is within the territory of Nigeria's Bakassi peninsula region and, with the provision of guns, a floating dock, and anti submarine net, it could be put into a state of defense. A first-class armored base could be built at Ambas Bay.

Duala, which is within the radius and territory of Nigeria's Bakassi region, however, could be quickly utilized not only as a base for flying boats and ocean-going submarines but also for other commerce-raiding crafts, including the 10,000-ton pocket battleships Deutschland, Admiral Scheer, and Admiral Graf Spee, which they built between 1933 and 1936. The three ships had max speeds of 26 knots. And the Germans had six eleven-inch guns on the 1938 diesel-engine, 26,000-ton battleships Scharnhorst and GneiSenau, which had a cruising range of about ten thousand miles and speeds between twenty-seven and thirty knots. These were recognized by British naval authorities as having been built for commerce raiding.

The Reich in Germany had commissioned five battleships with high speeds as against Britain, which had three that were not as modern. The Germans had retooled their industries, building advanced military weapons. It also launched the 35,000-ton battleship Bismarck, which carried eight fifteen-inch guns; a sister ship followed, and were all faster than any existing British ships, except three of Britain's battle cruisers, which were described by technical writers as offensive ships that in future war situations would not be confined to home waters.

The day the Germans launched the Bismarck in Hamburg, the Fuhrer decreed the widening and deepening of the Kiel Canal. The British realized that the few ships they had capable of speeds comparable to the German vessels could not be spared for duty in west African waters, and if one or two German raiders of this class were stationed there, they would be at an advantage if there was an outbreak of war.

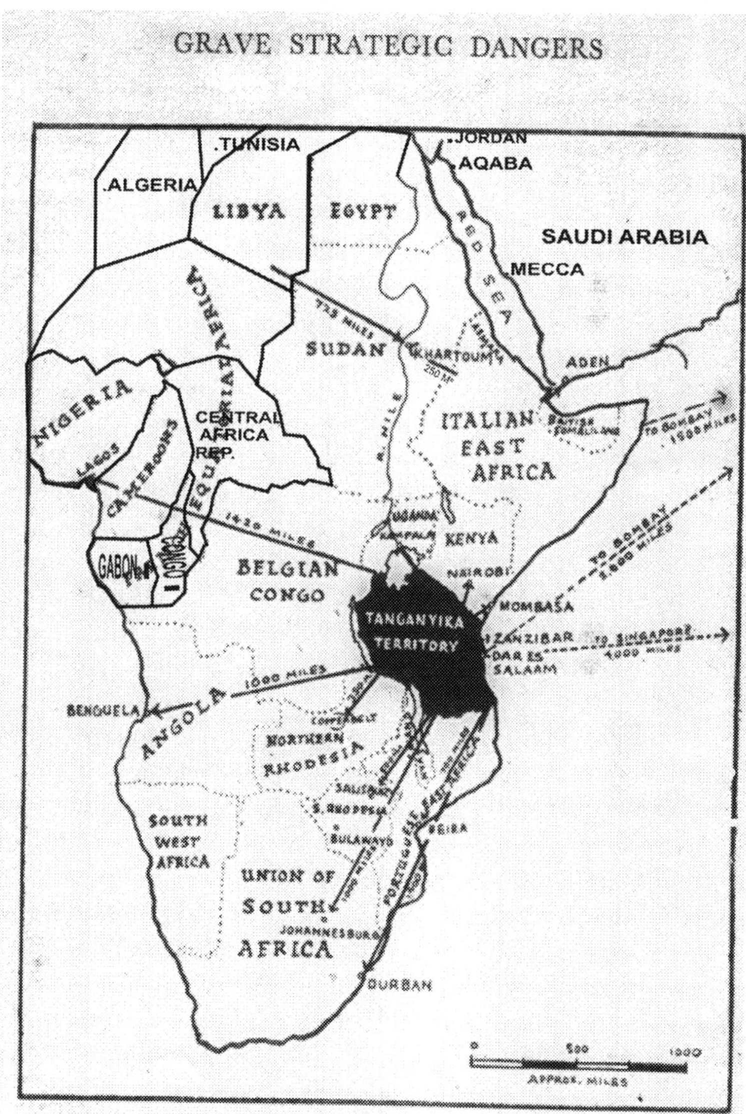

STRATEGIC DANGERS OF TANGANYIKA TERRITORY IF IN GERMAN HANDS

The British had suffered great damage to their shipping fleet by 1914. The shrinkage of their mercantile marine was reduced from 2,800 sea vessels to less than 1,800 by the end of the First World War and a loss of about 59,000 seamen. The commercial-carrying capacity of the 17.5 million tons was reduced to fourteen million tons, while the population of the British people on the other hand had increased drastically by about 4.5 million two decades after the First World War.

The British lost 2,098 seagoing ships and 578 fishing crafts. All this vessels were sunk during the First World War by German submarines, and at the peak of German offensive one out of every four ships that sailed from the British harbors was destined never to return. At this period, Germany had built 111 seagoing U-boats, but not more than one-third was estimated to be at sea at any given time. Germany, Italy, and Japan had about 270 submarines, with Germany having in secret dozens already built up in sections and ready for assembly. The joint striking power of their known strength was immensely formidable.

Hitler described the alliance as "the world political triangle," and it was believed at the time that their submarines and bombing aircraft could bring about a total blockade of Britain and France. With the institution of a convoy system, in which merchant ships are escorted by war ships, Germany having an African base would only magnify the problem.

The waters where the swift battleships of the Deutschland or Scharnhorst classes were at large, their eleven-inch guns and high speeds would, without risk to themselves, have easily sunk both the convoying and convoyed vessels.

The destructive capacity of these commerce raiders at the time was limited by the need to return to European harbors for fuel, docking, and overhaul. However, if refueling and all other necessaries had been available within the African territory at the time, which was still infrastructurally undeveloped, then their offensive power would be immensely formidable. This would have been possible by having African naval and military bases under the German flag.

Vice admiral C.V. Usborne, the former director of naval intelligence, had written at the time of the immense danger upon naval defense if African colonies were transferred to Germany. Unless France continued to work with Britain with new investments and expenditure on armament and military equipment running into millions of pounds, they could not match Germany with military capacity if it was given the African colonies to build naval and military bases.

The German vessels serving and plying the African and American routes were known to be capable of high speeds, considerably above those which they declared. The only purpose of the secret power reserve was intended for offensive operations in war. They were known as auxiliary vessels or cruisers. The German shipyards were building faster and bigger fishing trawlers and vessels with speeds of thirty-five knots and cruising range of 25,000 miles. History had shown that colonial powers could not maintain their overseas territories if they were weak in military strength. The 1935 and 1937 Anglo-German naval agreement had compelled Germany to reduce its military strength in proportion to that of Britain, who was the world's superpower.

Germany nearly won the First World War with its submarines and attributes being of great importance to them. But during the war it had used its submarines to fight other submarines, which was not the norm. Submarines do not attack each other. Germany's ability to disrupt the sea communications of other powers, particularly Great Britain, France, and the United States got them committed to invest more in military hardware.

During the hostilities of September 1938, German submarines were sighted at the South Atlantic and about thirty Italian submarines were known to be off the Somali Coast and within range of the Red Sea, making the Suez Canal a deathtrap. This threatened all ocean vessels on the Indian Ocean, which was almost a British lake. It was a major route the British used for import and export of goods, and half of the time one-fourth of Britain's mercantile vessels were afloat on the sea or at anchorage in its harbors, which made the Indian Ocean very busy with British ships. This situation had almost reduced Great Britain to a situation of famine during the First World War.

The Germans continued to arm Germany under Hitler's regime, and they built a new 10,000-ton cruiser named Seydlitz, which was armed with eight-inch guns. This terminated the "Cruiser Holiday" whereby the British had an agreement with Germany that it must not compete with the British armed forces either equipment-wise or in the number of servicemen.

Germany had breached all these agreements secretly and had planned to take the African colonies by force. By basing an adequate submarine fleet on a new German West Africa, incalculable damage could and would be done to shipping bound between the cape and Europe and South America, and Europe's two highly important sea routes for the provisioning of Great Britain and France. France had drawn manpower from its colonial territories when the need arose. The transport of troops was already threatened by German submarines in the Canary Islands, and the possibility of German submarine bases had made the zone very hazardous.

The Germans with their technical skills built new sophisticated submarines able to stay at sea for a four-month period with cruising speeds of 22.5 knots, as against other countries reaching 10–15 knots and staying submerged for eighty to one hundred miles at 4–6 knots. Germany had developed a new system of propulsion bringing higher speeds and lighter weight in construction with a total of 20,000-mile range.

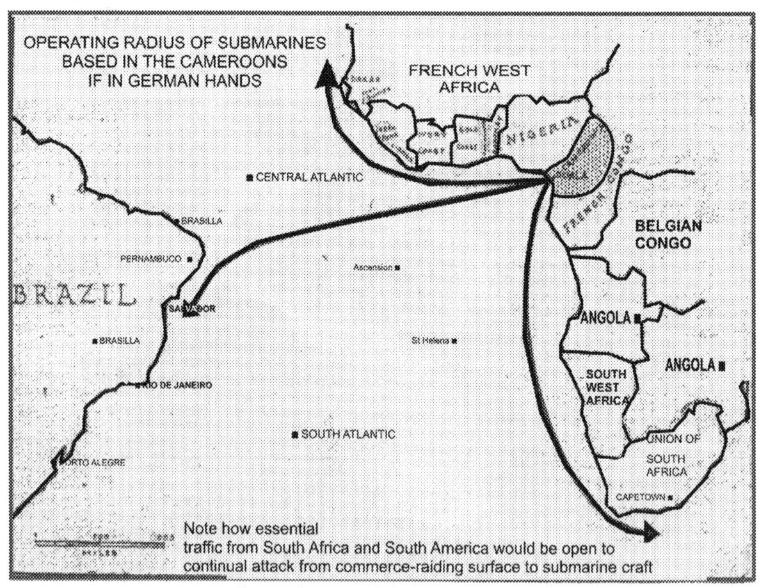

Italian submarines had the capacity to circumnavigate Africa with a normal fuel supply.

Cameroon is the farthest removed of the West African territories from the ocean, and it is just about 3,000 miles to Pernambuco on the coast of Brazil. So if, on assumption traffic from Asia, Australia, and south and east Africa had to be diverted to the Brazilian coast, underwater craft from Duala or other convenient West African lairs could journey across the South Atlantic and back and still have an operating efficiency of 9,000 to 12,000 miles. The range of submarines had, however, been improved, and the vulnerability of merchant shipping had not been reduced.

The United States got alarmed by Germany's demand for naval bases in Africa because of the bases being within striking range of Central and South America. America's own Atlantic fleet was based in Norfolk, Virginia, some 2,600 miles from the mouth of the Amazon.

The Atlantic Ocean had been the domain of the British as they controlled the waters while the United States monitored the Pacific Ocean. The United States felt that if the British had given in to the demand of returning the German colonial territories in Africa, the Monroe Doctrine could be challenged.

The British had known the Cameroon region to be very strategic to Africa and had felt that if a nation was willing enough to sacrifice machines, they could create havoc as the pilots could escape by parachute after performing the destructive duty assigned. Seaports, railways, dams, mines, towns, and other objective targets could be hit in west, central, east, and south Africa.

The British had stationed a squadron of Royal Air Force in Kenya, and Southern Rhodesia had trained pilots. But no matter how expansive the fighter and bomber jets, coupled with anti-aircraft equipment of British Africa, this could not prevent a German air force with African bases from accomplishing wholesale destruction and havoc. East Africa had at the time been accessible only by sea. This changed with the invention of the combustible engine. Germany continued to be dissatisfied with the Treaty of Versailles, which brought about National Socialism and the Nazi movement.

The treaty signed after World War I treated Germany very harshly, and this was greatly resented by the German people. Germany had lost territories in Europe and was forced to give up territories from its overseas colonies in Africa: Togo, Cameroon, Tanganyika (Tanzania, Rwanda, and Burundi), and Dar Es Salaam. The Germans were asked to reduce the size of their armed forces. They were then ordered to pay reparations that amounted to $33 billion as war damages because they provoked the war. These sanctions brought about grievances, and when the Great Depression came in 1929, Germany was affected severely. By the early 1930s, unemployment was at very high levels. Hitler now had to look for ways out where he decided eventually to defy all the charges made on Germany by the Treaty of Versailles. Hitler then rearmed Germany by building a massive army. He remilitarized the Rhineland, which this threatened the League of Nations as he then began to threaten neighboring states.[69]

Before the Second World War began, when Germany had failed to uphold the provisions in the Treaty of Versailles, the Great Powers, such as Britain and France, along with other members of the League of Nations, did not act by taking any actions to stop or put Germany in check. All they did was to refuse the return of the African colonies to Germany.

This emboldened Hitler's aspirations, and, by September 1, 1939, he sent troops into Poland. This led to formal declaration of war on Germany on September 3, 1939. Many European countries had scaled down their armies after the First World War and the depression years so they were easy targets for Germany to walk over and annex, such as Denmark. The League of Nations had the responsibilities of hearing international disputes and of mobilizing its members for collective action to enforce peaceful resolutions in the event of an aggression by any nation who attempted to breach the global peace.

The United States still held on to the policy of isolation, not venturing much outside its borders, and was not a member. The Soviet Union joined in 1935, but the league failed a major test in 1931 when the Japanese took over Manchuria and when asked by the League of Nations to withdraw they refused. This led to the resignation of Japan from the league. Manchuria was annexed and turned into a puppet state called Manchukuo. The league members were not in agreement of the steps to take, and the case died a natural death.

Hitler had rearmed Germany from the beginning of 1935. The Italian dictator Benito Mussolini began his invasion of Ethiopia, which he wanted for economic reasons, and the league used sanctions that failed. Britain and France tried to get a compromise settlement, but this failed as the Italians occupied Ethiopia completely by 1936. Ethiopia

69 http//wiki.answers.com/Q/what were the causes of world war 2

had never been colonized, and this was the first successful invasion from an outsider.

France had sought alliance with the USSR as Germany rearmed its military. This was an excuse that Hitler had used to arm the Rhineland in 1936. Britain and France had decided to keep the peace, but they later paid dearly for it when the Second World War broke out in 1939.

Hitler still campaigned for *Lebensraum* (living space), claiming Germany was overpopulated and needed space. He then annexed Austria in the month of March 1938. With the failure of a conference arranged by Britain and France with Hitler and Mussolini, Germany was given the go-ahead to occupy Sudetenland, which had been the last request of Hitler to maintain the peace. The war eventually still broke out as he disregarded all former agreements heading on his expansionist drive to conquer the world.

The world war broke out on September 1, 1939. Fascists support force and military power and feel it is acceptable in achieving national goals. Italy and Germans followed this path. The Germany under Hitler wanted to unite all peoples seen as *Germans,* bringing them together under one umbrella. This led to the crisis in Czechoslovakia.

Hitler had fears of Bolshevism and made it his life ambition to exterminate them. And the Jews were seen as the biological roots. Hitler had propelled himself to power by the Depression of 1929. The world powers got involved in the Second World War as a result of the following actions of the Germans.

Hitler invaded Poland, bringing in Britain and France to the war. Japan's takeover of Manchuria brought China into the war.

Japan attacked the US fleet at Pearl Harbor, bringing the United States into the war. Japan had for a long time been invading China en route to Korea. Japan had plotted to take control of Asia and the Pacific in a drive to emulate Western imperialism. The United States had put checks by placing embargoes on Japan. However, hoping to stop the United States from meddling in its affairs, Japan struck Pearl Harbor in a surprise attack to immobilize the United States. This action awoke the giant.

Germany invaded the USSR, bringing the Russians (Soviets) into the war. By 1945, it ended, and a bigger lesson had been learnt. This led to the formation of the United Nations.[70]

---

70 Ibid

Chapter Eight

America's Military Bases

After the end of World War II in 1945, the United States of America and the Soviet Union emerged as the two superpowers in the world. The United States operated democracy with the capitalist system of government while the Soviet Union had the communist and socialist system of government in place. Both states acted as watchdogs of the world in international affairs. The Soviets had invested huge amounts on an arms buildup and was the world's second largest exporter of oil. They squandered their enormous oil earnings in the 1970s and 1980s on military buildup and on a series of useless and, in some cases, disastrous international adventures. The United States was the number one oil exporter followed by the Soviets.[71]

But by the 1980s, both had reduced their output, and America opted for importing oil and gas from outside its shores, bringing Saudi Arabia to the front burner. The Middle East had taken over, and America became its biggest customer. The use of oil and its excavation process has brought about conflicts in many regions of world and has many times led to conflicts even within nation-states in the Middle East and Africa. Oil has become so strategic in the lives and economic emancipation of citizens and their nations. The demand for oil and gas by the world's industrialized nations has also shaped their international politics. Yet oil has also proved it can be a fool's gold. In some cases,

71 The Guardian, September 27, 2008, p. 45

it has brought financial growth without development, and, worse still, it has destroyed the badly needed virtue we all want to see around the world: morals. This has been Nigeria's major problem.

Nigeria is blessed abundantly with the wealth created from oil, but over the years it has only enriched the ruling class who refused to develop the nation to internationally acceptable levels. They rather bought homes overseas and kept the money offshore in personal bank accounts.

The shah of Iran was granted his desire as oil was discovered, but it later led to his dethronement.[72] The United States, once the largest producer, has still remained its largest consumer as it has to import, thus weakening its strategic position and bringing it into conflict with the current producer nations. This burdensome position has not been healthy for a superpower. Oil has played a strategic role in the politics of nations across the world. The Soviet Union eventually dismantled its communist economic structure in the late 1980s and has since then embraced democracy and the capitalist system of government, which is practiced by more than 90 percent of the world countries.

America from the 1990s became the only superpower in the world and has acted as gatekeeper, or is often referred to as "big brother of the world," which it has played well. The United States has worked with the United Nations, which replaced the League of Nations. The world's industrialized nations have permanent seats. They are the permanent members. After the world war, they went from G4, G5, G7, and now G8 member countries. The other countries of the world are signatories and members but don't fall under permanent member category.

The United States of America has been able to play this role of superpower with the help of its military bases that are within and outside its borders. America has done this through imperialism, which had been done by other countries more than a century ago.

America's military bases today are described and seen as the modern-day version of having colonies.[73] The United States dominates

---

72 Ibid

73 http://www.commondreams.org/view/04/0115-08.html, Chalmers Johnson, "America's Empire of Bases, Jan. 15th, 2004. http://guardian.co.uk/world/2009/August 27, Outcry in South America over U.S Military base pact

the world today through its military strength. The garrisons belonging to the United States encircle the whole planet.

A military base is a facility, settlement, reservation, or installation that shelters military equipment and personnel. A military base may also contain large concentrations of military supplies in order to support military logistics. These are restricted to the general public and only authorized personnel may enter them. Military bases provide housing, churches, gyms, recreational facilities, cleaning facilities, dining halls, etc.

A military base provides accommodation for a unit, but may also be used as a command center and a training ground or test ground. In many cases, the base relies on help from outside to survive. These are in areas of supplies of food and other daily needs all human being require to survive. However, certain complex bases are able to endure by themselves as they are able to provide food and water for the inhabitants.

The military base falls into four categories: air force bases, army and land bases, navy bases, and communication and spy bases. Britain had thirty-six naval bases at the height of its imperial zenith, the period it held the position of superpower of the world in 1898.

The Roman Empire was believed to be in possession of thirty-seven bases to police the regions from Britannia to Egypt and from Hispania to Armenia. Today the optimum number might be about forty bases for any imperialist aspiring to dominate the world.

However, today America's military bases are difficult to count. It seems nobody outside the system knows the exact number. The bases totaled 737 in other countries as of 2005, but there seem to be thirty-eight major ones. The data available from the year 2005 put it that the Pentagon officials value the bases at about $127 billion within the United States, and the value of all, including the foreign bases outside the United States of America, at a total of about $658 billion. It is believed the population figure of personnel employed is 1,840,062 military supported by 473,306 defense department and civil service employees, and 203,328 locally hired.

The overseas bases, according to the Pentagon, totaled 32,327 barracks, hangars, hospitals, and other buildings it owns and 16,527 more would be leased. The size was recorded from the inventory that covered 687,347 acres overseas and 29,819,492 acres worldwide, which makes the Pentagon the world's number one landlord.

It is believed there are more owned by the KBR corporation (formerly known as Kellogg Brown and Root) a subsidiary of the Halliburton group that maintains the bases. The figures do not include bases in Afghanistan or Iraq, which has about 106 garrisons as of May 2005, Israel, Kyrgyzstan, Qatar, and Uzbekistan, even though the US military has established colossal bases in Central Asia and the Persian Gulf since 9/11 by way of excuse. It is believed that facilities provided by other countries are not included. The sites don't include those of the Turkish government that are jointly used in collaboration with the Americans.

The Pentagon also does not include the $5 billion worth of military and espionage installations in Britain, which are classified under disguise as Royal Air Force bases.

There are some countries in the world who keep their American bases secret, fearing embarrassment if their defense pact with America was known and made public. The United States also has communication gadgets that can eavesdrop on others. That is why they often are able to tell when a coup or any crisis is going to happen in Nigeria and many other countries. Jordan and Kuwait have enjoyed defense pacts with the United States and can be viewed as satellite states.[74]

The United States government keeps a close watch on countries opposed to favorable trade relations with it. Washington stands by and would take on countries who work against the interests of the United States, particularly in South America like Brazil, Uruguay, and Guatemala, and Mexico in North America.

The creation of military bases should, however, not necessarily be seen simply in terms of direct military ends. They promote economic and political interests. The American multinational interests who deal in oil and gas have the interest in building a secure corridor for their pipelines from the Caspian Sea in Central Asia through Afghanistan and Pakistan to the Arabian Sea. The region has proven oil reserves. The war in Afghanistan, which brought democratic leadership with liberal and moderate ideas and the creation of military bases in Central

74 http://www.globalresearch.ca/index.php?context_va&aid=1284, Global research.ca by Chalmers Johnson

Asia, are viewed as strategic policies that will bring such pipelines into reality.

In the last years of the Bush administration, President George Bush fought the global war on terror (GWT) with the possibility of building military bases in Africa. The United States began negotiations with several of the African countries to install, buy, enlarge, or rent property for the purposes of getting military bases. Morocco, Algeria, Mali, Ghana, and Nigeria were on the favored list (AFRICOM). Africa's leaders, however, became suspicious and did not want any superpower within the territory that was colonized for centuries. Getting freedom from imperialist colonial masters and independence had not been easy. They did not want any superpower too close by, especially one that promoted democracy and democratic ideals.[75]

Africa is ruled by despotic leaders. Despite the democratic era finding its way into many of its states in the last decade, many of the nation states of Africa don't practice true democracy. Many call it a homegrown democracy that is operated to suit internal conditions of their various states. Most of the nation-states of Africa have been controlled by military rule for decades shortly after independence. The military has ruled Africa by decree, meaning most decisions are taken by a single person: the head of state or military. The many states of Africa operated feudal systems for centuries, and this still rears its head in the way the internal nations are governed. The ruling class controls everything with the help of state power and the followers who are the citizens.

However, considering all the wealth that has been generated by many of the states, few have hope of surviving. Many of the different states in Africa have the wealth of the nations in private pockets in overseas accounts and don't have much to show in terms of developmental infrastructures within the society and uplifting of their people.

America's current secretary of state, Hillary Rodham Clinton, visited a few of the African states shortly after the inauguration of President Barrack Obama and told many of the African leaders in a friendly and candid way about the failures in Africa. She put the blame on the bad management and corruption that had gone on for years in the continent. When she got to Nigeria, she spoke so nicely about the Nigerian state and its friendly citizens, but she had said what we all

---

75 www.newsafrica.net, News Africa, March 31st , 2008

know and complain about in the newspapers and our daily lives. What hurt the Nigerian government was that an outsider was telling them about all the ills going on in Nigeria. It was as accurate, as if Clinton was living in Nigeria and was a citizen. This brought her a standing ovation and applause.

Clinton said it in the best way an angel can rebuke the human race. I arrived in Nigeria and was disappointed when I saw that many parts of the country were in darkness. I expected a nation that has benefited immensely from oil as the sixth largest producer in the world should be electrified all over, but the ruling class has refused to let the money come down. They have kept the money at the top, within their class, and have not uplifted the masses of Nigeria.

America wants to help Nigeria and other African countries, but we must start by helping ourselves and the government paying more attention to infrastructural development. If a vote had been taken for election that day, she would have emerged the president of Nigeria. She delivered her speech the Nigerian way; no foreign envoy had ever been so charismatic, directly telling us the honest truth from the day Nigeria got its independence. Of course the government was not pleased. It was during the administration of President Umar Yar'Adua. They felt it was point-blank.[76]

The United States wants to have military bases in Africa for strategic, economic, and political reasons being that many of the African states have failed with continued conflicts more related to holding and sharing power. The power tussle in many African states has led to instability in the region, and, with the crisis in the Middle East, America wants to do business with more stable regions and countries. The reason is to keep the West stable by securing the stability of troubled regions.

Many of the African states have discovered oil, which makes the region attractive to oil-thirsty giants like the United States and China. The stability of the region is necessary for the stable supply of oil and gas for the United States consumption and European Union. In fact, all nations benefit from stable periods when there are no conflicts around the world. Conflicts drive up oil prices, and that is not good for Europe or America as it raises the cost of production and drives up the inflation rate on their economies, which they try to keep at stable single-digit rates.

76 The Guardian, August 13, 2009, p. 1

The stability of the region also reduces the number of migrants and refugees fleeing to Europe and America. The West often bears the brunt of conflicts in troubled areas. The reason is that everybody wants to go abroad to safer societies.

Africa has often been too far away that when there are political crises and problems like genocide going on, as we saw in Rwanda, Sudan, etc. The American government cannot do much because of the distance, especially when they don't have the military bases to use.

The leaders in Africa have realized this difficulty and do not want the United States within their borders. They feel the sovereignty of their countries will be threatened and that America might begin to meddle and dictate to them. It is a way to police leaders into good governance where the killings will have to stop. It will help reduce the barbaric wars that have taken place and will still happen if a system of checks and balances are not put in place by the international community.

The interest of the United States in having some African bases triggered uncomfortable reactions in Europe. The Europeans don't want America meddling or interfering with their former colonies, which they still oversee and have economic ties with. They regard the region as their sphere of influence.

The former president of Nigeria, Olusegun Obasanjo, had a hot romance with America from 1999, when he became the president of Nigeria. For the eight-year period, he was always running to Washington like it was just his country home. President George Bush and Tony Blair had a soft spot for him, and they always granted him audience. The chemistry flowed just perfectly. They were a kind of Three Musketeers. He was like their representative in Africa. The relationship paid off. Nigeria got debt cancellation.

The instability in the Niger Delta brought concerns to the Western governments, and this prompted the pressure for an American base. However, President Olusegun Obasanjo treaded softly and did not give the go-ahead. This romance with America affected the Bakassi Peninsula judgment in The Hague, whereby the International Court of Justice delivered the fraudulent judgment against Nigeria. It was a decision given to deter the American government from getting a base in the Bakassi region, a strategic military zone for any world power to occupy.

This brought the conspiracy to trigger Cameroon's agitation for the region. The European Union and Britain have been aware of this region for decades and do not want a superpower grabbing the forbidden region for military purposes, such as having a garrison and military base in the region. Then the international conspiracy started, using the French loyalist Paul Biya, who is currently the president of Cameroon.

The Germans had owned the Cameroons during the colonial days up to 1918 when the First World War ended. The League of Nations confiscated all German colonies when the Treaty of Versailles was signed. Cameroon was shared between France and Britain because they could not afford to have a superpower in the region with military bases that would put their nations at risk. Nobody in Europe could take the risk of Germany having control of the region. This was because its foreign policy was expansionist, militaristic, terroristic, and domineering of all weaker nations. The bases could be used for intrigue. Nobody among the world powers could afford bases of intrigue, especially around Duala in Cameroon or close to the Bakassi region.

As America remains the only superpower, and especially with the way George Bush had unilaterally invaded Iraq just a few months after a similar invasion of Afghanistan, where he was able to dislodge the Taliban government with ease, other countries became worried. Afghanistan was a region the Soviets could not conquer for years.

George Bush defied the United Nations and singlehandedly invaded Iraq using the unilateral approach as opposed to multilateralism. This got other world leaders, who saw another Nazi leader in the making, worried. The ICJ at the Hague had to defraud Nigeria. They just robbed Peter to save Paul.

Why should Nigeria lose its territory of Bakassi to Cameroon because America wanted a military base? I don't think this was a fair judgment, and if the ICJ at The Hague acted out in error, I might have titled the book *Error at The Hague.* But these are known facts. But the average on looker will say, "Oh! It's because of the oil in the region." Nigerians only look one way: the money spinner; the oil in the region. France was very antagonistic to America before the judgment. After 2006, President Chirac changed his anti-American posture with the Bakassi decision in favor of Cameroon. The French felt relaxed: no more threat of bases in Bakassi.

The network of American military bases is located strategically to the proximity of energy sources. This has brought political opposition and resistance from anti-war activists. Demonstrations against the bases have occurred in Spain, Ecuador, Italy, Paraguay, Uzbekistan, Bulgaria, and a few other countries. The objectives are sometimes to promote disarmament and sometimes environmental reasons. The Pentagon is, however, considering movement away from rich democracies like Germany and South Korea and looking more at poverty-stricken countries to move the American bases to, because of the easier and more permissive environmental laws and regulations.

The Pentagon has agreements with countries that host the military bases, a status of forces agreement that exempts the United States from cleaning up the environment where the bases are located. This brought grievances to the people of Okinawa, where the American environmental record has been nothing short of abominable.

President Bush in 2003 signed into law the Defense Authorization Bill of $401.3 billion, which exempted the American army from abiding by the Endangered Species Act and the Marine Mammal Protection Act. The military bases are important to many countries as they help boost local economies by providing jobs and inflows of cash. The bases also help America's domestic economy. For example, on the eve of the war on Iraq, while the defense department was ordering extra cruise missiles and depleted-uranium armor-piercing tank shells, it also acquired 273,000 bottles of Native Tan Sun block, almost tripling its 1999 order, which was a boost to the supplier Control, Supply Company of Tulsa, Oklahoma, and its subcontractor, Sun Fun Products of Daytona Beach, Florida.[77]

The American government had shown its interest in putting its military bases in some of the African nations, and this was under the name AFRICOM. Former President George W. Bush was the first American president to visit Benin in West Africa. He pledged $307 million in supplementary assistance from the United State Millennium Challenge Account (MCA) to alleviate poverty.

Critics, however, accused him of failing to address the poverty in Benin, blaming their woes on American subsidies to the American farmers who grew cotton. The American and European governments give subsidies to their farmers despite the fact that in 2004 the World Trade Organization had declared subsidies a violation of the global trade

77 http://www.commondreams.org/views04/0115-08.htm, Chalmers Johnson, America's Empires of Bases.

rules. That is the weakness of the African continent—not knowing how to convert its raw materials into finished products. Benin grows cotton and will not get good prices with subsidies in America and Europe given to farmers.

The United States government invested heavily in Africa under the Bush administration, attaining record levels with assistance given to tackle the HIV/AIDS problem, investing as much as $23 billion in 2006, also during the administration of President Bill Clinton of the United States in 2000 when the African Growth and Opportunity Act (AGOA), which had been introduced allowed duty-free access to the United States' market, meaning exporters from other countries who sent farm produce paid no duty. The cocoa farmers in Ghana and Cote d'Ivoire have benefited immensely from duty-free access as they supply major transnational corporations like Mars, Hershey's, and Nestle. These companies pay low prices to the farmers for their cocoa beans, creating a lower standard of living for the farmers.

How many African countries today manufacture chocolate? Those are the problems of Africa: the knowledge to produce finished products that can compete favorably with the European and Chinese goods. Rather than find a way to solve some of these problems by trying to develop a knowledge-based economy, Africans keep blaming Europe and America, saying they caused our woes.

President Bush at the time created an emergency plan for AIDS relief (PEPFAR) and invested $15 billion in antiretroviral drugs. In 2003, only 50,000 people in Africa had access to the drug, but by 2003 1.5 million were getting medicines to treat HIV/AIDS as a result of PEPFAR.

This was a major plus for the Bush administration. He succeeded in bringing Africa to the center of America's foreign policy. Even if the administration was attracted by oil, which is abundant in Equatorial Guinea, then it is still okay. At least the former president had used his initiative well. Bush, during his tenure, traveled to five African countries hoping to convince the African leaders on America's military command for Africa (AFRICOM). The move was rejected, raising a lot of dust on the international scene. The European Union (Britain, France, Germany, etc.) had remembered the forbidden zones on the coastal states in Africa, making Washington under George Bush halt the process.

America's invasion of Iraq in 2003 made countries question Washington's global security intentions when it unilaterally went ahead without getting legitimate international backing. This flouted the United Nations law whereby the majority needed to consent before such action could be taken.

America had sought military-to-military relationships with the fifty-three African nations, hoping that by 2008 the Pentagon would have established its AFRICOM headquarters whereby an African standby force would have been established. The move was seen as the beginning of militarization of Africa.

The opponents of AFRICOM had seen the move of creating military bases in Africa as America's global war on terrorism and also as an attempt to secure African oil supplies for the United States. The United States after the 9/11 attacks wanted to reduce its dependence on oil from the Middle East countries and wanted a secure relationship with Africa where there are huge reserves; Nigeria provides the United States of America 10 percent of its oil needs.

Paul Lubeck, Michael Watts, and Ronnie Lipschutz wrote a paper for the Washington-based Center for International Policy in which they argued AFRICOM was intended to spearhead the Pentagon's oil and terrorism policy, which would oversee the deployment of the United States' forces in the area (the Gulf of Guinea) and supervise distribution of money, materials, and military training to regional militaries and proxies. They added that, given the internal security problems often found in resource-rich countries, it was likely the newly acquired skills and equipment would be directed against domestic opponents instead of global terrorists. The United States gets 10 percent of its oil supply from the troubled Niger Delta region where there have been repeated shutdowns of oil fields.

The American government at the time of the Bush administration offered to assist the Nigerian government in stabilizing the region, which was reluctantly declined as critics raised fears that militarization of the region would further destabilize the region. The Nigerian government was cautious, fearing the loss of its sovereignty and also the causalities that would arise from such action. After all, they were the poor people frustrated by the government that over the years had neglected the region.

The people of the Niger Delta only fought for their legitimate right:

a better life and environment. The current arrangement in Nigeria, which produced a president from the Niger Delta minority region, has brought a change to the problem of the restiveness in the region.

It was under the Umar Yar'Adua/Jonathan administration that peace gradually returned. Having a vice president from the Niger Delta region eased the tension and also the amnesty program initiated by the government of President Yar'Adua.

Despite the shortcomings of AFRICOM and the refusal of the former President Olusegun Obasanjo to stabilize the region, many felt it was because he wanted the status quo to remain so that the price of oil could remain at an all-time high. This benefited the ruling class. It gave access to more funds, and the shut-down of Nigeria's refineries were deliberate actions and policies. The government wanted to import refined petroleum, which enriched the proxies used as fronts for the leadership. This was a lucrative gold mine. The electricity was shut down deliberately many times so that domestic consumption of fuel would rise. That is, fuel used domestically within Nigeria would increase, and once the consumption went up it would deplete the imported stock swiftly making the demand for fuel astronomical. This means that fuel imported to the country would be used up very fast. This will lead to them making new orders at a faster rate. They almost destroyed Nigeria.

The discipline and strong resolve of Nigerians to keep the peace has stabilized the nation. This has kept the country from disintegrating into a war zone. The refineries had created jobs in the Niger Delta, and, once they were not functional, all the jobs that were enjoyed by the Niger Delta people in the form of small contracts like cleaning and the few supplies that kept the blue-uniformed jobs (factory workers) and junior workers contented disappeared leading to the lucrative militancy and kidnapping and chaos that gave the country a bad image.

Another argument that was used for the need to have the American military base was that coastal African countries did not have the capacity to protect their territorial waters from the illegal fishing going on there, and that most African countries were losing billions of dollars from the trade.

However, despite the shortcomings, America and Africa continue to have joint military cooperation. African soldiers receive training in the United States. Over 44,000 African peacekeepers from nineteen countries have been trained by the United States. The United States partners with African states and 90 percent of peacekeepers are American trained. They are deployed to the African Union and United Nations, inside and outside Africa.

Africa is being moved into a central strategic partner and the Africa standby force put in place by the African Union has failed in its objectives to quell conflict within the African region. The case of Sudan, the Darfur crisis, and Chad are recent examples, and older examples are Rwanda, Burundi, Liberia, etc. Not much was achieved. It took years to restore peace.

The crisis in Cote d'Ivoire is a recent example. The country had elections on November 28, 2010. The incumbent president, Laurent Gbagbo, lost to the opposition rival Alassane Quattara, but he refused to accept the results. Laurent Gbagbo has served two terms but still does not want to leave. The leaders of the ECOWAS countries advise he should step down, along with the United States, former colonial master France, and the African Union, but he refuses.

He ordered the United Nations peacekeeping force to leave, but they refused. Nigeria shut its embassy, and the French government asked citizens of France to leave the country as sanctions began. The world looked on to solving the crisis and didn't want to allow greedy leaders to destabilize the country.

The world blamed America for looking the other way. It was George Bush who looked at the idea of having American military bases through AFRICOM. He felt this would bring faster solutions when there were conflicts, and this would probably keep the peace. The AU has not been able to bring rapid solutions to conflicts because it is not well equipped and needs more personnel to do such jobs.

Pentagon officials have argued that the only way America can get involved in stabilizing the region in times of conflict is with the help of the bases. Equipment and manpower would be stationed and ready to mediate conflicts.

Many African countries may be independent, but quite a lot of them still need a lot of guidance on conflict resolutions and management. The leaders still need guidance on how to run a state that is secular with different ethnic, religious, and cultural beliefs. They need to know when to compromise or back down on a repugnant law or policy. They also need to have the spirit of accepting defeat in elections.

Many African leaders are too greedy and always want to be in office and power. The era of sit-tight presidents should be abolished as we move along into the second decade of the millennium years.

Chapter Nine

Fraud at The Hague

The Bakassi territory had never been part of Cameroon, whether you go back to ancient historical books or not. Bakassi is a part of the Nigerian nation and has never had anything to do with Cameroon. Bakassi as an entity was in existence as far back as 1450, and the area was inhabited by the Efik people of southeastern Nigeria.

Historically, Bakassi is the peninsular extension of the African territory of Calabar into the Atlantic Ocean and is incorporated within the political framework of Calabar kingdom in Nigeria. It is currently bounded by Cameroon to the north and Nigeria to the south.

However, the historical events that led to the scramble and partition of Africa by European powers led to the signing of a treaty by Queen Victoria, simply called Treaty of Protection, with the king and chiefs of Calabar on September 10, 1884. This agreement, according to historical facts, enabled the United Kingdom to exercise control over the entire territory of Calabar, including Bakassi. Hence, the oil-rich peninsula became part of Nigeria, although the border was never permanently delineated.[78]

The Southern Cameroons voted in 1961 to leave Nigeria and become a part of Cameroon. It was a costly mistake they have not

78 http://en.wikipedia.org/wiki/bakassi, Bakassi-wikipedia, the free encyclopedia.

fully recovered from. The Bakassi people remained in Nigeria under the Calabar administration.

Bakassi is a land largely occupied by the people of Cross River state and Akwa Ibom state of Nigeria. The three major tribes in the area are the Efik, Annang Ibibio, and Oron.

Bakassi had been administered by the Nigerian government and enjoyed a significant degree of autonomy under traditional rulers. The last monarch of Bakassi was Etinyin Etim Okon Edet, an Efik man of Nigeria. Bakassi is situated at the extreme eastern end of the Gulf of Guinea and is a fertile fishing ground comparable to pollution-free areas in the United States and Scandinavia. The Bakassi Peninsula is commonly described as "oil–rich," though in fact no commercially viable deposits of oil have yet been discovered. The area has aroused interest from oil companies in light of the discovery of rich reserves of high grade crude oil. About eight multinational oil companies have participated in the exploration of the peninsula and its offshore waters.

France was among the world powers that owned colonies in Africa. Britain and France had an alliance and often worked together politically, economically, and internationally. The Germans owned Kamerun, which is now called Cameroon. But during the outbreak of war in 1914 and its end in 1918 the Germans had almost won the war due to its U-boats and the strategic position of its colonies in Kamerun and Tanganyika (today's Rwanda, Burundi, and Tanzania). It was during this period of war that the world powers realized the risk involved of having a superpower controlling those zones of the world.[79]

At the end of the First World War, in 1918, the colonies of Germany in Africa were seized and Germany was made to pay fines. This was from the Treaty of Versailles where the League of Nations served as the body similar to the United Nations. Then, with the outbreak of the Second World War and its end in 1945, it was decided that no superpower would be allowed to have bases in Africa because of the threat it posed to the commerce of other nations in Europe who got their raw materials from the African region. It was the knowledge of the waters around Bakassi toward Duala that was the forbidden zone.

The British knew this, and the French and the Germans also knew

79 F.S Joelson Germany's claim to colonies, Hurst and Blackett, ltd., June 1939.

about the strategic position the region had for a superpower to occupy. The Germans were a superpower during the first and second world wars and had to be barred from gaining control of those territories that posed a risk to the safety of other world powers.

The French waited patiently for the world's attention to be focused elsewhere and then the conspiracy started for the French to have control of the region through Cameroon, which acted as a satellite state for France in Africa. The president had been loyal, and they kept him in power as one of the sit-tight rulers. They ignored the long period he stayed as Cameroon's president because he did their bidding. They forgot democracy, the rule of law, and free and fair elections, and left him as president.

Then Paul Biya of Cameroon started his disputes with Nigeria. Cameroon and Nigeria on the fifteenth of May, 1981, 1991, 1993, and 1996 had almost come to the brink of war over the disputed peninsula. The Cameroon national radio at the time reported that a Nigerian military patrol violated Cameroon's territory by infiltrating the peninsula as far as the Rio del Ray and opened fire on the Cameroon army. Cameroon, it was reported, returned fire, killing five Nigerian soldiers.

Again in 1992 and 1993, the Cameroon government openly killed some Nigerian civilians in Cameroon stemming from multiparty democratic government and growing militarism for Anglophone autonomy. It was a period other Nigerians were forced out of Cameroon during tax-drive victimization. The Bakassi dispute intensified with two other major incidents that had provoked shootings, bringing death casualties to both Nigeria and Cameroon. Also in 1994, and from January to May 1996, there were border clashes involving military personnel. Diplomats reported by May 1996 that more than fifty Nigerian soldiers had been killed and some were taken as prisoners.

Southern Cameroon had claimed Bakassi as its territory. But why is it occupied and administered by Nigeria and why are all facilities that of Nigeria? Some conflicts continued in the region up to June 21, 2005, when Nigerian troops fired rocket-propelled grenades at a Cameroon security post, which killed one Cameroonian solider.[80]

---

80 http://www.america.edu/ted/ice/nigeria-cameroon.htm, Felicia price-The Bakassi Peninsula. The border dispute between Nigeria and Cameroon, November, 2005.

The conflicts went on for a few decades and then President Paul Biya of Cameroon went to court. The Ambazonians of Southern Cameroon feel more linguistically linked to Nigeria, and feel they are the rightful owners of Bakassi because they believed they were removed from that land under numerous transfers. This is an absurdity; nobody removed them. The world powers merely took control of the region. It was first under Germany, and then Britain and France took control of certain regions—they did not move anybody. There were merely demarcations and the Bakassi region fell under British control along with Nigeria.

The people that inhabit and live in an area are the owners of such territories regardless of changes of colonial master.

The Efik people who are Nigerian today have always been the occupants at Bakassi, and the Europeans met them there on arrival.

There was another border conflict around the Lake Chad area at the other end of the two countries' borders. The conflict, which started a few decades ago around the 1980s, eventually resulted in Cameroon, with the full backing of France, heading to court.

Cameroon had taken the matter to the International Court of Justice on the twenty-ninth of March, 1994. The International Court of Justice at The Hague in the Netherlands relied largely on the Anglo-German correspondence dating as far back as 1885, as well as treaties between the colonial powers and the indigenous rulers in the area, particularly the 1884 Treaty of Protection.

Cameroon pointed to the Anglo-German treaty of 1913, which defined spheres of control in the region, as well as two agreements that were signed in the 1970s. The 1975 Maroua Declaration between Cameroon and Nigeria was when General Yakubu Gowon was then head of state. Nigeria had a civil war between the Ibos of the east and northerners. The Ibos wanted to secede from Nigeria but did not succeed, and it cost a million lives. It was then that Gowon sought the help of Cameroon. Gowon sent strong memoranda to Cameroon on the advice and recommendation of Ahmadu Ahidjo, head of state of Cameroon, for strategic military cooperation during the civil war.[81]

He wanted Cameroon to block and secure the territorial waters of the region so that the blockade would prevent weapons from coming to Nigeria so that this would diminish the strength of Biafra.

---

81 Punch Newspaper, October 12th, 2002- Olumide I "Letter from the attorney general of the federation to the ministry of external affair"

However, after the war, the federal government had not instructed the Cameroonian government to retreat, and they continued to be within the Nigeria territorial waters, which gave them the false belief the territory was their own, that Gowon gave them Bakassi. The Maroua Declaration was not ratified by the Supreme Military Council, which means it is not valid.

It was this event that made Cameroon officials believe the region around Bakassi belonged to them. It has been one of the flaws of Nigeria having leaders that did not pay attention to the leadership responsibility given to them. This comes from the top to bottom: the presidency, the governors, and local government chairmen. This has been the weakness of Nigeria. We as a people have not paid attention to certain aspects of our lives and nation as a whole. Our interest lies more in personal enrichment, and we are still inexperienced.

The surveyor general's maps had omitted Bakassi. These are, however, forgivable elements due to the backwardness of the African nation. Many maps used today are still the ones done by the British. We were just a decade into independence; most of the nationalist leaders knew nothing about running a country effectively. In fact, fifty years after independence, many African nation-states grapple with the successful management of running an effective state.

Many of the African states have ended in chaos and have become failed states politically, economically, and socially. Nigeria had gotten its independence along with other African states too early. It was not yet ready for independence but nationalists with their paper certificates had felt they could manage a country. Few had tried, but many had no clue to building a nation.

The International Court of Justice based its finding basically on the 1913 Anglo-German agreement that sovereignty over the territory belonged to Cameroon. The international court then instructed Nigeria to transfer possession of the oil-rich peninsula to Cameroon but was silent on what should be done with the inhabitants. Were they to change nationality or retain their Nigerian status as citizens of Nigeria?

In 1994 precisely, Cameroon asked the International Court of Justice (ICJ) also known as the World Court, to settle a dispute over its boundary with Nigeria, especially the question of sovereignty over the Bakassi Peninsula, and over islands in Lake Chad, and to specify the course of the land and maritime boundary between the two countries.

After an eight-year period, the court delivered its judgment on the supposed merits of the case on the tenth of October, 2002. It decided, in part, that sovereignty over the Bakassi Peninsula and the disputed area in the Lake Chad region belonged to Cameroon.

This judgment was a fraud at The Hague.

The European superpowers have known for over a century the strategic importance of Bakassi as a region. The region is a danger for the nations of world if any superpower controlled the region with military bases. The region was forbidden for military bases and garrisons because it could be used for intrigue. It could cause a blockade for commerce and shipping of any kind and could also be used as military outpost for striking other nations around and far away.

The British, French, Belgian, and German governments are well aware of this fact. The European continent as a whole has this information. It was because of the Germans and their expansionist and militaristic stance and approach to its neighbors and other nations that it was barred after the First World War from the region. This was the decision reached by the League of Nations. African military bases would not be tolerated by members of the League of Nations, as it would pose a danger for all Europe and Asia and the world at large.

The military posture of President George W. Bush in his fight against terrorism, which he promoted globally after the terrorist attack on the United States on September 11, 2001, and his unilateral decision to invade the sovereign state of Iraq without the full approval and support of the United Nations brought about the international conspiracy.

The European Union had to keep him out of Africa, especially Nigeria, which the Europeans saw and still see as their "colony." Britain did not want America meddling with its former colonies, especially Nigeria where a wonderful relationship had existed for years and was being rekindled.

The president of Nigeria at the time was very close to George Bush. In fact, he was like Bush's "African cousin" since former President Obasanjo of Nigeria was a regular guest in the United States. The Europeans felt that if he gave the nod for a military base to be established, Bakassi could be used.

This prompted the judgment against Nigeria from all evidence that was presented and further discussed; the reader by now should not have any doubts. Plans to invade Iraq were being discussed at the period the judgment was given. The issues surrounding the Bakassi Peninsula had turned out to be an intense struggle between truth and falsehood. Nigeria was so bombarded with falsehood that it became virtually impossible to discern the truth. Nigeria was bullied and intimidated into abandoning the security of the frontiers of its borders and the welfare of its people, which is the very essence of governance and the country's sovereignty and nationhood.

President Obasanjo had consented to prejudgment conditions in a closed-door meeting convened by the French president, Jacques Chirac, and this did not imply the collective will of the people of Nigeria. It is not binding in international diplomacy and international law.

This cowardice by a president who not only was forced on Nigerians but came in the guise of a born-again Christian paraded himself as the most "patriotic" of Nigerians, which clearly underscores Nigeria's state of quandary.

The decision at The Hague on the tenth of October, 2002, led the secretary-general of the United Nations, Kofi Annan, to mediate and chair the tripartite summit with the two leaders on November 15, 2002.

The outcome of that summit was the establishment of a commission to facilitate the peaceful judgment. The aftermath of the decision got the presidents of both countries, Paul Biya of Cameroon and Olusegun Obasanjo of Nigeria, to find a way to implement the decisions of the court. They had asked the secretary-general of the United Nations, Kofi Annan, to set up a Cameroon-Nigeria mixed commission chaired by the secretary-general's special representative for west Africa, Ahmedou Ould-Abdallah, to consider ways of following up on the International Court of Justice ruling and moving the process forward. In 2003, Nigeria began the gradual process of withdrawal. This agreement became known as the "Green Tree Agreement." The ICJ judgment was backed by the United Nations whose charter potentially allowed sanctions or even the use of force.[82]

Another meeting had taken place on the thirty-first of January, 2004.

---

82 http://www.un.org/news/press/docs/2006/sgsm/0511.doc.html, Secretary General at signing ceremony, June 12th, 2006. Cameroon

The leaders of the Bakassi people had threatened to seek independence if Nigeria refused to keep the territory. Their protest was ignored and not heard. On the thirteenth of June, 2006, Nigeria's president, Olusegun Obasanjo, and President Paul Biya of Cameroon were said to have decided to resolve the international impasse at the peace meeting held at the insistence of Kofi Annan in New York City.

It was then that Nigeria started the gradual withdrawal of its 3,000 troops on the first of August, 2006, and a ceremony on the fourteenth of August marked the formal handover. However, on twenty-second of November, 2007, the senate of the federal republic of Nigeria rejected the transfer of the Bakassi Peninsula to Cameroon, citing constitutional defects in the Green Tree Agreement signed by President Olusegun Obasanjo with Cameroon, contrary to section 12(1) of the 1999 constitution.

This also led to the decision of a high court in Abuja, the federal capital of Nigeria, giving a verdict of noncompliance with The Hague judgment. The high court in Nigeria declared that before the government at the center could go ahead with the handing over, certain aspects of the 1999 constitution, which recognized Bakassi as one of the 774 local councils in Nigeria, must be amended to suit the new development.

Another federal high court had restrained the federal government from ceding Bakassi to Cameroon. Justice Mohammed Umar had ordered that all parties to the suit, including the federal government, should maintain the status quo. The justice of the case was that all parties involved in the suit should maintain the status quo so that the subject matter won't be destroyed. The subject matter was southern Bakassi.

More than 75 percent of the population of Nigeria was in support of Bakassi being in Nigeria, but many only thought it was about the oil deposits believed to be in the region. There were, however, notable Nigerians who readily asked the government to hand it over and give the region away. I wonder what kind of Nigerians they are, those who work against the state, especially those in the legal field. Their actions are treason.[83]

– Nigeria Boundary Agreement crowns remarkable experiment in conflict.

83 Sunday Vanguard, December, 2nd, 2007, Oladele, Bakassi's Senate action breaches international law obligatio

The former attorney general of Nigeria and minister of justice, who recently got his title the "senior advocate of Nigeria" revoked for obstruction of justice in cases related to corruption and embezzlement, was among the Nigerians who urged the government to hand over its territory. Chief Michael Aondooaka (SAN), minister of justice and attorney general of the federation, declared that whatever judgment that was delivered at the high court was not strong enough to stop the handing over because the World Court at The Hague was higher than any court in the land. He declared, "Besides different judgments have been delivered on the matter by two different courts, so I choose the judgment to obey and the one not to." He added that "Nigeria will obey the International Court of Justice ruling that ceded the disputed Bakassi Peninsula to Cameroon."

Many more lawyers, including Joe Kyari Gadzama (SAN), also said that, because Nigeria was a respected member of the international community, this made it mandatory for it to honor its obligations. He had said Nigeria should give its territory away for a membership of the United Nations Security Council. He said further that if not, the country might face sanctions from the United Nations if it violated the agreement on Bakassi. One begins to wonder when some Nigerians will stop the habit of a bribe to get something or a prominent position. Being a member of the United Nations Security Council is by merit; countries have to earn it.

Another notable Nigerian made utterances shocking enough to question his qualifications as chief of naval staff. Did he get to the position by merit, or was he assisted to the post through a certain network of connection and loyalties? This was the chief of naval staff, Admiral Ganiyu Adekeye. He said Nigeria should give the peninsula to Cameroon, a weaker neighboring country flexing its muscles while being a satellite of France, on the grounds of friendliness. And in order not to attract sanctions from the United Nations.[84]

Prince Bola Ajibola of Nigeria and Abdul G. Koroma were two of the judges that gave dissenting opinions to the judgment. Four others who agreed with the lead judgment gave dissenting opinions on some aspects of the judgment.

Prince Ajibola of Nigeria voted against the decision of the judgment

---

84 Daily Independent, Michael Jegede, August 7th, 2008.

concerning Lake Chad and Bakassi Peninsula. He declared the judgment political.[85]

Another notable Nigerian was radical lawyer Richard Akinjide, a former attorney general and minister of justice who had declared that the judgment was 50 percent international law and 50 percent international politics. This was blatantly biased and unfair, a total disaster and complete fraud.[86]

Three important issues emerged from the Bakassi saga. The first was the implication and consequences that would emerge from the Green Tree Agreement. The second was that Nigeria's armed forces were not consulted. The army, navy, and air force were not involved in the negotiations that led to the signing of this agreement. The military had objected, saying the agreement undermined the security of Nigeria.

The third important issue was the presidency under Obasanjo, and his successor the late president Umar Yar'Adua had both failed to submit the Green Tree Agreement to the national assembly for ratification. The legislature failed in its oversight function to call the president to order. The national assembly, the House of Representatives, passed a resolution requesting the president to seek national assembly ratification before completing the transfer.

They were ignored, which they readily accepted! What should have been done was to take serious actions by bringing impeachment proceedings, which was the only opportunity they had to impeach the president. Usually when they did make this move, it was about their financial gains of wanting increased allowances or the French Peugeot 607. When it tickled their fancy and furniture allowances, a lot of hue and cry went into this matter, and the president granted them the desire.

The people of Bakassi, not knowing what to do or how to fight the case, issued all sorts of threats to no avail, including filing a case of contempt against the attorney general of the federation and asking to be independent of Nigeria.

The former chief of defense staff during the administration of former president Obasanjo, General Martin Luther Agwai, had accompanied

---

85 http://www.gasandoil.com/goc/news/nta24467.htm- Alexanders Gas & Oil connections news and trends Africa, October 30th, 2002.

86 The Guardian, September 27th, 2008, Richard Akinjide, "How oil and gas are used in the games of nations".

the president at the time to New York but was unable to give further details of the military's involvement and contributions. The successor to General Martin Agwai was General Andrew Azazi. He was very bold and behaved like the high-ranking officer that he was. He told the committee on public hearing that the military was not consulted and no details of input were given. He said he had yet to lay hands on any document prepared by the military over the matter. He was very annoyed at the time and only tried to hide his disgust at the last hour by trying to speak in a diplomatic way. General Azazi told the committee on public hearing that boundary adjustment in Bakassi Peninsula, if left the way it was by the fraudulent judgment at The Hague would jeopardize Nigeria's security because of the Calabar ports. He further disclosed that it would undermine Nigeria's shipping capabilities, as the deep water is now mostly on the Cameroon side from the way the judgment was given.

The then chief of naval staff Andrew Azazi stated the flaw in the judgment. He said section 4(d) of Annex I of the agreement states Cameroon shall allow innocent passage in territorial waters of the zone to civilian ships sailing under the Nigerian flag consistent with the provision of this agreement, to the exclusion of Nigerian warships.

Azazi lamented the boundary commission talked about an agreement that was written in 1975, and we are talking about a document signed in 2006 that says our warships can only operate up to certain levels. He was talking of the strategic Calabar Channel, which is about twelve nautical miles. The agreement divided the channel into two, ceding the right side to the east, which is the deep water part, to Cameroon and the left side to the west, which is shallow, to Nigeria.

He further asserted that it was of deep concern to the army if we as Nigerians cannot go through the deep waters; it means Nigeria cannot make any movement. Our big vessels will be landlocked and unable to sail through. The agreement was designed in a way that compromises Nigeria's security because Nigeria's water channel to Calabar had been ceded to Cameroon. The implications of the judgment for Nigeria are many. It means the Nigerian navy can no longer protect the open sea to Calabar.

After five years from August 14, 2008, both navy and merchant ships can no longer go there without the permission of Cameroon. That will be in 2013. In a national emergency, Cameroon may likely refuse the request. The Cross River State's Efik people are losing their homeland where the British met them when they arrived on the shores and islands of the country eventually called Nigeria.

The state government will also lose the expected international maritime traffic when Tinapa opens. The Calabar free-trade zone will be affected. Recently, the Cameroonian government started asking for the multibillion Naira Tinapa resort in Calabar. What effrontery! I would like to state here this point: can Cameroon, all on its own, without the mischief of France, dare to challenge Nigeria? The Security Council will have to look at the matter again as presented.

In spite of any flaws that might have arisen from the legal team at The Hague representing Nigeria, the plot and conspiracy had been hatched for a long time. Keeping Nigeria out of Bakassi is securing the area against the American military base under the AFRICOM initiative.

Nigeria had been in physical control throughout the many centuries as the place is home to the Efik people. Nigeria administered it. There were hospitals, police stations, post offices—everything you can see in a modern state was provided by Nigeria. Cameroon never had possession. In fact, it was believed Cameroon's border began from a nonexistent river. When the old boundaries were delimited at the time of the partition of Africa, geographical knowledge was inexact and the ethnographical factors were not understood (pg. 172, Germany's claims to colonies). The decision of the International Court of Justice at The Hague can be described as imperialism at its worst. Nigeria was in control of Bakassi and Cameroon was never in possession, and thereby was not in a position to claim the territory. The crux of the matter is that you cannot transfer a territory and the people without the right to self-determination.

The World Court, also known as the ICJ at The Hague, was presented with the following treaties and points of arguments, which led to the final decision of the French judge, Gilbert Guillaume. He awarded the disputed territory of Bakassi to Cameroon on October 10, 2002.

- The 1884 Anglo-Efik Treaty;
- The 1885 Anglo-German Treaty;
- The 1913 Anglo-German Treaty;
- The 1975 Maroua Declaration between Nigeria and

Cameroon; other legal issues from the judgment are privities of contract, ratification, registration, consideration, judicial precedents, the right to self-determination, etc.;

- The law of treaties;
- The Vienna Convention, under article 26 on the law of treaties, 1969.

Every treaty in force is binding upon the parties and must be performed by them in good faith. This is the statutory provision of the long-established and cardinal customary international law principle of *pacta sunt servanda.* This had been defined as agreements are to be kept, treaties should be observed. Pacta sunt servanda is the bedrock of the customary international law of treaties and according to some authorities the very foundation of international law. Without such an acceptance, treaties would become worthless.

Thus, the 1884 Anglo-Efik Treaty is a binding agreement between Britain on the one hand and the Obong, chiefs, and people of Calabar on the other. Accordingly, anything done by either party in breach of the terms of that treaty violates not only Article 26 of the Vienna Convention on the law of treaties but also the fundamental customary international law principle of pacta sunt servanda.

During the case concerning Bakassi and Cameroon the advisory opinion in relation to Western Sahara case, the International Court of Justice pointed out that in the period of 1884, before, during, and after the advent of the colonialists from Europe, neither the Bakassi Peninsula nor any other part of Efik territory was virgin land that belonged to anybody or state. The Bakassi Peninsula and other parts of the Efik territory had long been under effective occupation, and this granted ownership to the Efik people who for centuries had formed social and political organizations that were controlled by the leadership of the Obong.

Henceforth, the Europeans, the British specifically, could not have automatically acquired ownership and sovereignty over any part of Efik territory by occupation. The occupation of weaker nations by stronger ones did not confer title on the annexing state as such territory was already occupied by people referred to as *the natives* of the place.

The 1884 Anglo-Efik Treaty was for protection and friendship only. It was not a cession treaty. Therefore, that treaty did not cede

Efik territory to the colonial masters, nor did it confer ownership and sovereignty on regions including Bakassi.

This in effect meant that the 1884 Anglo-Efik Treaty, both original and derivative title over the entire region referred to as Efik territory, lay and still belong to the Obong, chiefs, and peoples of Calabar. And since the treaty did not transfer or purport to transfer title to the British, the ownership of Bakassi belongs to the Efik people of Nigeria who had always lived there.

The 1861 treaty between the British and King Dosumu of Lagos had been a cession or subjection treaty, but, even after the First World War, the African colonies had been taken from Germany. The members of the league, including Britain and France, had said they did not own the colonies and were in control of them to assist the natives who were being trained for future self-sustenance and independence. This meant they kept the colonies as trustees pending *when* they were asked by natives to give the colonies full independence. This, Britain and France said, had no fixed time, as they would need to train the inhabitants of the region to meet up with the advanced world.[87]

The Anglo-German Treaty (1885)

This was a treaty signed between the colonial masters Britain and Germany, the details of which are stated as follows.

"Germany engages not to make acquisitions, accept protectorates, or interfere with the extension of British influence in the coast of the Gulf of Guinea lying between the right river banks of the mouth of the Rio del Rey." The British also made a similar undertaking to Germany. The principles applicable in pacta sunt servanda apply to the 1885 treaty, as they do to other treaties.

The International Court of Justice made the 1913 Anglo-German Treaty the basis of its judgment. This can, however, be faulted on several political and legal grounds. It violates the fundamental principles of international law, which are codified under article 26 of the Vienna Convention on the law of treaties and the maxim pacta sunt servanda.

Firstly, there was already in existence a valid treaty: the 1884

87 Daily Independent, pc7 pc9 exact words used, Okanga ogbu Okanga, Bakassi and the validity of treaties

Anglo-Efik Treaty. The provisions stated the British had undertaken to protect the Obong, chiefs, and peoples of the old Calabar region, including Bakassi. If, however, the British had entered into agreement with another group that is not native to the place, which was the treaty entered with the Germans. The action can be seen as stabbing the Efik people in the back thereby purporting to cede the Bakassi Peninsula to the Germans. This was and is still a gross violation of the 1884 Anglo-Efik Treaty and contrary to the letters of Article 26 of the 1969 Vienna Convention on the law of treaties.

Secondly, there existed the 1885 Anglo-German Treaty, which established the Rio del Rey as the boundary separating the spheres of influence of Britain and Germany. It prohibited both countries from acquiring or interfering with each other's territory, which they referred to as *spheres of influence.* It was and remains a breach if Germany truly signed a treaty with Britain in 1913 with the view of acquiring Bakassi, which was already under the British government and its sphere of influence.

In signing the 1913 treaty between Britain and Germany, they had not acted in good faith. And since there was already a subsisting and binding treaty, the Anglo-German Treaty of 1885, which had forbidden both world powers from acquisition of each other's spheres of influence, it leaves me wondering.

However, since it is on record that Britain and Germany did not ratify the 1913 Anglo-German Treaty, what then is the effect? The effect of non-ratification of treaties is provided in the cases of Nicaragua v. US.[88]

The 1913 Anglo-German Treaty has no effect because both countries did not get their parliaments to have it ratified, which made it nonbinding. And this means the treaty is not binding on Nigeria and Cameroon under the principle of state succession.

If we go further here, after the hostilities of the First World War, which ended in 1918 and the confiscations of German territories in Africa, which was effected by countries that formed the League of Nations who had defeated Germany and made it sign over the ownership of its African colonies, how would we now relate the past treaties signed between Germany and other powers? Will they still be binding? I feel

88 Ibid

all German agreements and rights ended when colonies were taken in 1918, so former treaties and rights were nullified at that time.

Furthermore, the 1913 Anglo-German Treaty can be questioned on its relevance and validity because it was not registered. The validity of non-registration would arise with either the League of Nations or the United Nations that supplanted it.

In Article 80 of the Vienna Convention on the law of treaties 1969, it states that "Treaties shall after their entry into force, be transmitted to the secretariat of the United nations for registration or filing and recording as the case may be and for publication." Article 102(2) of the United Nations charter stipulates no party to any treaty or international agreement, which has not been registered in accordance with the provisions of paragraph one of this article, may invoke the treaty or agreement before any organ of the United Nations.

The League of Nations had similar provisions in its Article 18. The purpose of registration is to give publicity to the treaty and its content and also to avoid secret treaties.[89]

By the principle of *nemo dat quod non habet,* Britain could not legally cede the Bakassi Peninsula region to Germany under the 1913 treaty because Bakassi did not at the time, and also now today, belong to Britain. This principle was applied with approval in the Island Palmas case but was rejected in Nigeria v. Cameroon by the International Court of Justice at The Hague.

This was done because George W. Bush had unilaterally gone against the United Nations and world powers by invading Iraq.

They saw a Nazi regime resurrecting itself in America. They all became jittery as America remains the only superpower left in the world; it has a number of military garrisons and bases around the world and sophisticated military equipment like the surveillance, communication, and intelligence work being performed by unmanned aircraft and satellites. It also has sophisticated missile defenses like the ground-based Patriot Advanced Capability-3 and sea-based Standard Missile-3, which are used to protect US troops overseas. Also the deployment of a long-heralded system designed to protect the US homeland against long-range missiles. The Unmanned Aerial Vehicles (UAVs), the drones are some of the sophisticated weapons United Nations has.

Other US weapons include the air force's Predator and Global

89 Ibid

Hawk; the army's Hunter and Shadow; and the marines' Dragon Eye, the Phraselator-like hand computer that translates foreign languages; water, land, and air drones; sophisticated ocean vessels and submarines; and robots like Andros, PackBot and Matilda that go into caves and search tunnels. The United States and its ally, the powerful and sophisticated Israel, have too many weapons. The no-nonsense posture taken by George Bush after 9/11 made world leaders uneasy around the globe.[90]

The invasion of Afghanistan and the defeat of the Taliban regime within days sent shivers around the world. The debate on Iraq was going on when the ICJ made its decision. America was still planning to invade Iraq.

Then, as al-Qaeda and the Taliban got their foothold into the African continent through the north of Africa, and with the genocide in Rwanda, Burundi, Sudan, and other conflicts that were ravaging Africa, this led to the escalated refugee problems and migrants coming into Europe and America. The world blamed America for not caring about Africa. This prompted George Bush, the hero of the first decade of the millennium years, to seek ways to help Africa. Washington wanted to have a strong foothold in Africa to check the despotic leaders in the region who had often put their countries on a path of conflict, failures, and mismanagement, which led to power struggles between groups within and between African states.

However, after the lengthy periods of self-government and independence spanning a period of fifty years, all is still not well, and many of the independent African states have become failed states as a result of bad leadership, corruption, and mismanagement leading to ethnic conflicts. Africa has been surviving on aid from the developed countries. Many of the African states are rising from the ashes and rubbles of war-torn states. Chad, Sudan, Liberia, Sierra Leone, and Somalia are examples.

The United States president had shown interest in the idea of having military bases in Africa under the Africom program. (America's military command for Africa.) This idea came about because the African Union could not deal with the conflicts and genocide in Africa by coming together to stop the conflicts. It was Nigeria, through General

---

90 http://www.therewatlantis.com/publications/the paradox of military-technology, The new Atlantis

Babangida, that had started the ECOMOG forces who are peacekeeping forces, but not much was achieved as some stubborn African leaders and dictators refused the African Union from interfering in conflicts within their states. Thousands is an understatement. *Millions* have died in the various conflicts that have taken place in the region, and Europe and America bear the brunt as refugees flock to their borders. It also destabilizes the raw materials and energy sources that serve the West, such as oil, gas, copper, diamonds, gold, tobacco, and uranium.

The British, French, and Germans have had the knowledge of the strategic regions in Africa that are forbidden areas for a superpower to hold fort. The reason is that they could be used as hotbeds of intrigue, a danger to other world powers. These strategic positions are in Bakassi and today's Rwanda, Burundi, and Tanzania, all too close or within the German African territories of Cameroon and Tanganyika. However, Bakassi is so near the Cameroon border and close to Duala.

This was the danger and threat seen over one hundred years ago. This resurfaced recently, which led to the conspiracy at The Hague to defraud Nigeria of Bakassi.

The Nigerian government had always been close to the United States president and Washington, and because of this the world powers had plotted to gain control. France, on discovering America had become a lone superpower, decided to get the Bakassi region by using the World Court and the president of Cameroon, which is a satellite state to France. They brought conflicts with Nigeria, which would lead to the court cases and the decision at The Hague in favor of Cameroon.

The principle of *privity of contract* can also be invoked to fault the validity of the 1913 Anglo-German Treaty. Under the doctrine of privity of contract, only parties to a given contract are bound by it. Thus, strangers or third parties are not bound by it and do not derive any benefit from the contract.

At the international level, only parties to treaties are bound by them and derive benefits from such treaties.

Accordingly, the Anglo-German Treaty of 1913 ought to be binding only on the parties (i.e., Britain and Germany). The Obong of Calabar, the chiefs, and people of old Calabar were not parties to the 1913 treaty. Rather they were strangers to it, thus exempting them from it. This means the Anglo-German Treaty of 1913 is also not binding to Nigeria as it was not a part of it. There was no country called Nigeria then. Nigeria emerged in 1914. Treaties do not create either obligations or right for third parties.

The Maroua Declaration (1975) is not valid because it was never ratified by the Supreme Military Council (SMC). The letters of Article 11 of the Vienna Convention of the law of treaties, the North Sea continental shelf cases, and Nicaragua v. US are invoked to challenge the validity of the Maroua Declaration. Cameroon claimed to have registered the Maroua Declaration in 1981 at the UN secretariat (registration No. 19976) and published in the United Nations treaty series. It is herein submitted that the registration of a treaty that is invalid *ab initio* does not and cannot confer validity on such a treaty. You cannot put something on nothing and expect it to stay there. Certainly it would collapse as held in Mcfoy v. UAC Limited. Cameroon was wrong to have done so unilaterally. A valid bilateral treaty ought to be registered bilaterally by both parties concerned and not by one of the parties with the absence of the other.

This makes the Maroua Declaration invalid because Nigeria did not join it to register it. A non-ratified and invalid agreement done at the United Nations secretariat nullifies it. One party or state cannot make it a legal document.

In the Bakassi case where the Cameroon government took Nigeria to court at The Hague, the judges that handled and decided the case were from Britain, France, and Germany. They sat on the ICJ or World Court panel. Judge Guillaume is a French national, Carl August Fleischhauer is a German, and Judge Higgins is an Englishman. As citizens of France, Germany, and Britain, which are the originators of the conflict between Nigeria and Cameroon and which still have vested economic and political interest in their former colonies, the judges should have excused themselves. For the three judges to have participated in the Bakassi case between Cameroon and Nigeria, in which their home countries have substantial and manifest interests, they have acted as judges in their own causes.

Nigeria still has the opportunity to act within a reasonable time. The maxim of equity is that equity aids the vigilant and not the indolent. Whoever wants to act must do so within a reasonable time.

The case was contrary to judicial precedents for example in Western Sahara (supra).

The court recognized the local rulers' possession and title as superior to other forms of title. But in the case of Bakassi, with similar fact to the Western Sahara, the same court refused to recognize the original title of the kings, chiefs, and people of Calabar and relied instead on the 1913 Anglo-German Treaty.

The judgment at The Hague violates the right of the people of Bakassi to self-determination.

Articles 1 and 55 of the United Nations charter provide for the right to self-determination of all human beings. The ICJ judgment that Bakassi sovereignty lies with Cameroon tried to make Nigerians Cameroonians and also denied them their right to self-determination. The illegality of transferring people from one territory to another without their consent is illegal, as is chasing them out of their territory.

The security council of the United Nations has to review the case. They need to take the political step of correcting the fraud committed at The Hague. The need for a referendum to decide what the people want or where they want to go is not necessary. The ICJ judgment at The Hague was given to favor Cameroon in order to keep the United States of America out of Bakassi.

It was President Umar Yar'Adua who handed over Bakassi to Cameroon as his predecessor, Olusegun Obasanjo had instructed to do. This questioned his motives. The handover and compliance by the presidency had been a one-man decision. Bakassi is a part of our constitution in the first schedule and sections 8(4) and 9(3). The president had breached the constitution, committing impeachable offences by supporting the lawlessness of his predecessor, irredeemably rubbishing his supposed commitment to the rule of law. The national assembly failed in its duty to serve the interests of the Nigerian state. They should have impeached the former head of state, President Obasanjo from the onset, and when his successor wanted to implement the illegality they should have risen to the occasion to impeach him. I guess self-interest overruled the move, and the implication of Goodluck Jonathan, his vice-president at the time becoming Nigeria's president. Goodluck Jonathan was vice president to president Umar Yar' Adua and when the latter died he became the president.

The emergence of Goodluck Jonathan as president of Nigeria was turbulent, the kingmakers up north of Nigeria "had their hands tied".

The north of Nigeria had lost the zonal agreement in the political arrangement in Nigeria through the ruling political party, PDP.

The agreement was for a southerner to have eight years maximum at the presidency and a northerner the same. The American presidential system of government is what operates in Nigeria's democratic government. However, the power sharing is not enshrined in the constitution of Nigeria. It was a political party's decision. The agreement was flawed because Nigeria is technically Five zones; the north has the Hausa and Fulani ethnic groups, which divides it into two. The middle belt who form another zone have the Igala, Idoma, etc., ethnic groups and the south, which has three zones and three ethnic groups. The Yorubas in the southwest, the Igbos in the southeast, and the Niger-delta people who are the Ijaws, Itsekiri, Urhobo, etc., form the south-south.

The people of the Niger-delta area currently produce oil in Nigeria. The Niger-delta region has never produced a president for Nigeria.

President Goodluck Jonathan is from the Niger-delta and is the first vice-president and president from the Niger-delta region.

The ruling elite north of Nigeria, however, felt cheated. The north had only done two years in the new arrangement and power was going to the south again. They wanted the president to complete the first four-year term of the north and stay out of the presidential race, which would have allowed the north another four-year term. This would have completed the eight-year slot maximum the political party had agreed on.

This, however, did not happen, and the current president of Nigeria, Goodluck Jonathan, who emerged through the demise of the late president from the north got a tremendous support not seen in Nigeria for decades. He became like a colossus and since the north had produced the president for thirty-five years out of Nigeria's fifty years of independence. The majority backed him for the April 2011 elections in Nigeria, which he won.

President Goodluck Jonathan has promised lots of changes if elected into office for a single four-year term. He is a gentle man but might not be able to fight corruption in Nigeria.

President Goodluck Jonathan would have to take the step within the international community to reclaim Bakassi as Nigeria's territory.

Treaties, even when in compliance with section 12 of the

constitution, cannot controvert the supremacy of our constitution or circumvent it. The former presidents, both Olusegun Obasanjo and the late Umar Yar'Adua, had failed to consult widely and had acted unilaterally as if the nation belonged to them. You don't give out territories unilaterally without consulting the relevant agencies in Nigeria. This applies worldwide.

Bakassi belongs to Nigeria, and the United Nations Security Council must look into the matter and return the region to Nigeria.

Bibliography

Books

1. Anene JC, The International Boundaries of Nigeria. The framework of an emergent Africa Nation London longman 1970.
2. Dowden Richard, Africa Altered states ordinary miracles. Great Britain Portobello books ltd. 2008
3. Gunther John, Inside Africa Hamish Hamilton ltd London 1954
4. Joelson F.S Germany's claim to colonies Hurst and Blackett, ltd, June 1939
5. Lawal O.A. O level government of West Africa Ibandan educational books (Nigeria) ltd. Heinemann educational books, 1982
6. Meredith Martin, The state of Africa; A history of fifty years of independence, Great Britain free press, 2005.

Periodicals

1. African Business, July 2006
2. BBC focus on Africa, July-September, 2006
3. BBC focus on Africa, January-March, 2009
4. Daily Independent, August 7, 2008
5. Daily Sun, March 30, 2010

6. News Africa, March 31, 2008
7. New African, Summer 2007 "Our Course is Africa's Cause" Zimbabwe special report.
8. Newsweek, March 1, 2004
9. Newsweek, January 31, 2005
10. Newsweek, July 31, 2006
11. Newsweek, special edition/issue 2008
12. Newsweek, special issue, "How to fix the world", December 2008-Febuary 2009.
13. Sunday Independent, December 27, 2009
14. The Africa Report No 16, April-May 2009
15. The Economist July 31st, 2004
16. The Economist February 19th-25th , 2005
17. The Economist July 16, 2005
18. The Economist August 6, 2005
19. The Economist August 5, 2006
20. The Economist September 2nd , 2006; Special report, September 11th, 2001
21. The Economist June 9, 2007
22. The Economist October 4th-10th, 2008
23. The Economist April 11, 2009
24. The Guardian, September 27, 2008
25. The Guardian, July 30, 2009
26. The Guardian, August 13, 2009
27. The Middle East, July 2006 (Pan-Arab Magazine) "Arabs wage war on money laundering",
28. The Nation, August 1st, 2009
29. The Nation, August 5th, 2009
30. The New York Time Magazine, April 2, 2006
31. The Punch, October 12, 2002

32. The Punch, August 4, 2009
33. The Punch, January 8, 2010
34. Time, December 31st, 2001/January 7, 2002
35. Topic Issue No 132
36. Vanguard, October 12, 2002

WEBSITES

1. http://www.guardian.co.uk/world/2009/aug/27/anger-america-columbia-bases-deal.htm. Guardian.co.uk. Outcry in South America over U.S military base
2. http://www.commondreams.org/views04/0115-08.htm. Chalmers Johnson, America's empire of bases, January 15 2004, Tom Dispatch.com
3. http://www.globalresearch.ca/index.php?context/va&aid=12824. Global research Ca by Chalmers Johnson 737 U.S military bases global empire.
4. http://encyclopedia.Jrank.org/articles/pages/5926/africagermancolonies.html. African German Colonies
5. http://africahistory.about.com/od/eracolonialism/a/scramblewhy-2.htm. What caused Scramble for Africa?
6. http://wiki.answers.com/Q/whatcausedworldwar1.html
7. http:// wiki.answers.com/Q/whatwerethecauses-of-world-war-2
8. http:// www.un.org/news/press/docs/2006/sgsm10511.doc.htm. Secretary General Cameroon-Nigeria boundary agreement crowns remarkable experiment in conflict prevention says secretary general at signing ceremony.
9. http://www.urhoboland.com/comments/diesode/the%20loss%20of%20bakassi.htm. The Loss of Bakassi.
10. http://www.nigerdeltacongress.com/articles/bakassi-remains-nigeria's-territory.htm. Bakassi Remains Nigeria's Territory
11. http://www.gasandoil.com/goc/news/nta/24467.htm. The World Court Rejects Nigeria's Claim To Bakassi

12. http://legalopinion.blogspot.com/2007/12/bakassi-senates-action-breaches.html. Law and Politics
13. http://en.wikipedia.org/wiki/bakassi. Bakassi-Wikipedia the free press encyclopedia
14. http://www.time.com/time/world/articles/08599,1937041,00.html
15. http://www.american.edu/ted/ice/nigeria-cameroon.htm. Inventory of conflict and environment (ice) Bakassi Peninsula
16. http://africanhistory.about.com/od/eracolonisation/p/mandateafrica.htm. Mandates In Africa About.com African history
17. http://www.thenewatlantis.com/publication/the-paradox-of-military-technology. The New Atlantis. A journal of technology and society
18. http://www.globalresearch.ca/index.php?context=va&aid=5564. The worldwide network of U.S military bases. The Global Deployment of U.S Military Personnel. Professor Jules Dufour
19. http://www.infoplease.com/ce6/history/Ao861782.html. Treaty of Versailles in world war I.